Refugees at Work

Compiled by
SOPHIA M. ROBISON

with a prefatory note by
ELEANOR ROOSEVELT

Published for
THE COMMITTEE
FOR SELECTED SOCIAL STUDIES

KING'S CROWN PRESS
NEW YORK, 1942

PREFACE

The study on refugees was undertaken by the Committee
for Selected Social Studies at my request, in the hope
that the findings would serve to answer the countless in-
quiries that were made of me concerning the refugee, and
whether he did or did not constitute the threat to American security -- economic and other -- that many feared
him to be.

It was my desire to secure completely unbiased sponsor-
ship. The American Friends Service Committee was asked to
sponsor the study, and it was arranged that the Committee
would work under the auspices of Columbia University.

The study in New York showed a considerable group who
had transplanted skills to America and, instead of displacing Americans were employing them in new trades.
There, also, proved to be groups who were employed in
necessary jobs in the service industries but, at very
nominal wages, so that family incomes were no larger than
those of their American neighbors, although there were
sometimes as many as three or four wage earners in the
family.

Among the refugee group there was no evidence of any
lackadaisical attitude. They were found willing to do
anything that needed to be done, and to accept the situation in which they found themselves. They have, in a
sense, been so long in the presence of a war situation
that their attitude is one that might often serve as an
example for our own conduct now that we are ourselves at
war.

I hope that this study will be widely read so that it
may allay the fears of those who are now making it more
difficult for the refugees to make a real contribution
to their new homes, through fear of competition when
there may be a new lag in employment.

PREFACE

It seems more and more evident to me that this group will be helping us to revise our economic system and to find new ways of keeping people employed at a high level.

We are fortunate indeed to have some of the best trained minds of Europe among us now as citizens and we should welcome them and use them to the limit.

Eleanor Roosevelt

TABLE OF CONTENTS

TABLES

INTRODUCTION

OCCASION FOR THE STUDY

The impact of the new refugee on American economic life
has given rise to prejudices of many kinds, some favorable.
But basic data have not yet been gathered or presented
which give adequate answer to the two groups which seek
information on this subject. On the one hand, there are
those whose pity has been aroused by the plight of the un-
fortunate victims of Nazi persecution and who wish to aid
them reëstablish themselves in America; and, on the other
hand, are those who wish to appraise the economic effect
of America's hospitality to these newcomers who, at first
glance, would seem to offer only competition to hard-
pressed older Americans.

To answer all the questions that these two groups raise
assumes omniscience in regard to the workings of our economic system.

THE SOURCES OF THE DATA

While data are provided by the records of the Bureau of
Immigration and Naturalization as well as by the records
of the unofficial agencies set up to aid the refugee (immigrants who since 1933 have come to America with the intention of settling here from countries dominated by
Hitler), these sources do not reveal, for example, how
many of Czechoslovakia's former manufacturers have set up
business in Chicago or Baltimore; how many Austrian lawyers peddle groceries or neckties in Philadelphia; nor
the number of German housewives who work as domestics in
New York City households.

The published tabulations of the Bureau of Immigration
and Naturalization distinguish alien immigrant from alien
non-immigrant, correlate country of birth or race with
country of last permanent residence (six months' or more
duration) and former occupation, classify immigrants by
sex, age groups, marital status, literacy, port of entry,
state of destination, whether they were arriving to join
relatives, and whether or not they "showed" more or less
than $50 to the immigration officials.

When the records of the Alien Registration Bureau are finally available, it will be possible to sort out for each year since 1933 refugee aliens by country of birth and by occupation, as well as by present residence.

While the files of the refugee agencies record the stories of the newcomers who came for advice, employment or financial aid, they rarely carry beyond the point at which the refugee becomes self-supporting. In addition, they have no data on the probable large number who never asked for aid.

No one of these sources tells how the newcomer got his foothold as entrepreneur, peddler, farm hand, physician, mechanic, teacher -- an important factor in his acceptance in a highly competitive labor market. Did he use the usual channels for employment, or was he placed through an agency specially created to solicit jobs for refugees? Did he use the favorite source for better jobs, i.e., the recommendation of friends? When he got his job was it assumed that a job for a foreigner should yield less than the usual wage? All these conditions affect the acceptance of the newcomer in America.

Full answer to these questions would mean person-by-person tracing of each of the almost 150,000 refugee immigrants who came to America between 1933 and June, 1941, and would presume extensive resources in money, time, and staff.

THE AUSPICES AND STAFF OF THE STUDY

The Committee for Selected Social Studies, under whose aegis this study was begun, was formed through the interest of Mrs. Franklin D. Roosevelt with Miss Agnes King Inglis as Secretary. The study of Refugees at Work was undertaken by this Committee with the coöperation of the Social Science Department of Columbia University. The necessary budget was made available to Columbia from a variety of sources, no one of which sought to influence the findings.

An Advisory Committee consisting of Professor Robert M. MacIver and Professor Robert S. Lynd of Columbia University, Mr. Clarence E. Pickett, Executive Secretary of the American Friends Service Committee, and Dr. Sophia M. Robison, of the part-time faculty of the New York School of Social Work, was appointed to supervise the work, which began February 15, 1941 and was brought to a close August 31, 1941.

Mrs. Emmy Crisler Rado, with a wide acquaintance among newcomers from all countries, assumed administrative direction. With Miss Inglis, Secretary of the Committee, she made arrangements for finance, office space, equipment, the recruiting of adult volunteers, contacts with business groups, and for the studies in Boston, Chicago, Philadelphia, and Baltimore.

Mr. Gerhart Saenger, author of Today's Refugees, Tomorrow's Citizens,* who was engaged to carry on the study, supervised the student field work in New York City. Mrs. Sophia M. Robison, as volunteer technical consultant, advised on planning the study and on schedules. From May 15 on she took responsibility for directing the study. She wrote the manuscript.

Colleges in New York City, Baltimore, and New London** agreed to grant some academic credit to well-qualified students majoring in the social sciences who volunteered their services as interviewers. Their performances were objectively rated on specially prepared schedules, recording the time spent, the number of calls, and the quality of the performance. This plan provided for the services of 130 students. Only three students dropped out, one because he obtained employment. All but one student earned academic credit. Effective part-time use of students required great flexibility in programming, considerable patience, and careful supervision by Mr. Saenger.

THE SCOPE OF THE STUDY

The study was conceived in two parts: The first, to ascertain from the individual refugee what type of jobs he obtained, through what channels they were secured, and what relation they had to his age, his stay in America,

---

* Harper and Brothers, June, 1941.
** Barnard College, Brooklyn College, College of the City of New York, Columbia University, Hunter College, New York School of Social Work, New York University, Queens College, Goucher College, Johns Hopkins University, and Connecticut College for Women.

his family situation, and his training or occupation abroad; and the second, concerned with those enterprises organized by refugees, to discover the fields in which they operated, the number of employees, both Europeans and Americans, and the extent to which they introduced new skills or new products.

The study of individual vocational adjustment was in the main confined to New York City, the mecca of more than 60 percent of all immigrants in the last decades. Supplementary individual studies were made in Baltimore and New London County, and supplementary studies of refugee enterprises were made in Baltimore, Buffalo, Chicago, Newark and its environs, and in Philadelphia. These cities were chosen because they are among the main centers of refugee settlement, and because interest and personnel were available. The tabulations for each of the studies were made from schedules sent to the New York office and a mimeographed report containing tables and explanatory text which covers method as well as findings is available upon request.

THE COOPERATORS

In any study as comprehensive as this one, the coöperation of a large number of persons is necessary. This study was fortunate in the amount and quality of the volunteer effort. Among the persons who gave generously of both time and service were Mrs. Arthur M. Rosenbloom and Mrs. Sumer Singer, who did a large part of the interviewing of the owners of refugee enterprises. In the office Mrs. George Bell, administrative director of the Dutchess County Study, Miss Millicent Baker, Mrs. James Egan, Miss Eve Felddegen, Mrs. Michel Sciapiro, performed many tasks for which budget allowance would otherwise have had to have been made.

Newcomers to America who donated their services as statistical assistants were: Dr. Arnold Coutinho, Mr. Simon Gallewski, Dr. Erich Grave, Dr. Stefanie Guttman, Dr. Fannie Kaplan and Mr. Hirsch Meiksins, both formerly of Documentation de Statistique Sociale et Economique, Paris, Mr. Fritz Oppenheim, Dr. Paul Schick, and Miss Marie Wolff.

The United States Committee for European Children loaned office equipment and Miss Caroline Flexner and Mr. Sylvan Hanauer were helpful in other ways.

Among the out-of-town organizations which made this study possible were: In Baltimore, the Baltimore Council of Social Agencies, Miss Anne D. Ward, Executive Secretary; and the Jewish Family and Children's Bureau, Miss Edith Lauer, Executive Secretary. In Boston, the Boston Committee for Refugees, Mr. Walter Bereinger, President; and the New England Christian Committee for Refugees, Mrs. H. Epstein, Executive Secretary, assisted in carrying on the Boston study. In Philadelphia, the Jewish Welfare Society, Mr. Joseph Beck, Executive Secretary, coöperated with Dr. Hertha Kraus of Bryn Mawr, who selected Mrs. Irene Tugend-reich, to carry on the Philadelphia study and secured the services of Mrs. Irene Gruenberg for the Chicago study.

Special interest groups such as the American Association of Former European Jurists, Dr. George M. Wunderlich, President; International Student Service, Victoria Schrager and Josephine Lee, Secretaries; the Emergency Committee in Aid of Displaced Foreign Scholars, Dr. Laurenz H. Seele, and Miss Betty Drury, Executive Secretary; the Jewish Agricultural Society, Dr. Gabriel Davidson, General Manager, cooperated by opening their files to the study.

The officials and staff of the Division of Immigration and Naturalization of the Department of Justice, and the Alien Registration Bureau, Washington, D. C., made every effort to make available the necessary data for the background of official statistics needed in the preparation of the report.

Nationality groups represented by such organizations as the New World Club, Mr. Fred H. Bielefeld, President; Mr. Siegfried Aufhaeuser of the Labor Committee for Immigrants from Central Europe; as well as Mrs. Hilde Scott, Employment Bureau; and the Prospect Unity Club, Mr. Herbert Steinhauser, Manager, were of major assistance in reaching the German refugees.

The Austrian American League, Dr. Otto Kallir, Chairman; the Italian Refugee Club, Dr. Fausto Pitigliami, Secretary; the Masaryk Club, Joseph Stein, Secretary; the Netherlands Jewish Society, Mr. Alex S. Boekman, Secretary; and the Cultural Association of Polish Jews, Miss Selma Steinman, Secretary, provided access to special nationality groups. The Immigrants Conference, Dr. Wilfred

C. Hulse, Executive Secretary, was the medium for reaching some professional groups. Access to the working class group was made possible through the American Labor Educational Service.

New York City organizations with special interest in the refugee problem as, for example, the Ethical Culture Society, Dr. James Hart, Director of Refugee Activities; the International Club of the West Side Young Men's Christian Association, Mr. Harold Page, Director; the Young Men's and the Young Women's Hebrew Association of Washington Heights, Mr. Samuel Solender, Director; the Young Women's Hebrew Association, Mrs. Ray F. Schwartz, Director; the National Board of the Young Women's Christian Association, Miss Mabel Brown Ellis, Secretary of the Committee on Refugees, helped in many ways.

Special mention must be made of the wholehearted coöperation of the agencies and committees which form part of the National Refugee Service, Inc., Dr. Albert Abrahamson, Executive Director. Specifically, Mr. Lawrence R. Klein, Director of the Department of Information and Statistics and his assistant, Mr. Robert Pasternak; Mrs. Stella E. Baruch, Director of Personnel and Office Management; Mr. I. Hosiosky, Secretary of the Capital Loan Committee; Mr. Edward B. Marks, Jr., Director of the Division for Social and Cultural Adjustment; Mr. Harry D. Biele of the National Committee for the Resettlement of Foreign Physicians, were available for consultation whenever advice was sought. Among other Board members of the National Refugee Service, Mr. Erich M. Warburg, was generous in giving time and assistance in making contacts with the out-of-town committees. Mr. Frederik Borchard, of the Joint Distribution Committee, made suggestions in connection with the coverage of enterprises in this study.

Acknowledgment has been made at appropriate places in the text of the work of the students and the faculty of the colleges which coöperated in the interviewing. Special mention, however, should be made of the advice and assistance of Professors Agnes Byrnes and Bernhard F. Riess, both of Hunter College; of Dr. Gladys Meyer, Student Project Advisor of the New York School of Social Work; of Professor Samuel S. Joseph, of Dr. Heinrich Infeld, of Mr. Joseph C. Markowitz, all of the College of the City of New York; of Professor Belle Zeller of Brooklyn College; of Professor Dan W. Dodson of New York University; of Professor Willard Waller and Dr. Mira Kamarovsky of Barnard College; of Professor Bessie Bloom Wessel of Connecticut College for Women; of Professor Lloyd G. Reynold, Department of Government, Johns Hopkins University, Baltimore, Maryland; and of Professor Elizabeth A. Redden, Department of Sociology, Goucher College, Baltimore, Maryland.

At all times during the study, Dr. Manfred George, Editor of the Aufbau, and Dr. Joseph Maier, Assistant Editor of the Aufbau, gave assistance through the columns of the their publication.

Mr. Harry Lurie, Director of the Council of Jewish Federations and Welfare Funds, Inc., Dr. Abraham Harris, of Howard University, and Dr. Otto Nathan, of New York University read portions of the manuscript and offered critical comments.

Finally, to the refugees themselves who were patient and coöperative in filling out the questionnaires, the debt of the study is immeasurable.

Not all of the data available in any of these studies are presented in the sections which follow. The files presented rich veins for future probing.

I

AMERICA'S REFUGEE POPULATION

It is neither possible nor important in relation to the major purposes of this study to know all the characteristics of the new immigrants. What is important, however, is their number, their distribution in various parts of the United States, their varying backgrounds in such terms as country of origin, occupation, sex, and age, and the period of entry into this country. These data, available in the tabulations published and unpublished of the Bureau of Immigration and Naturalization* furnish the criteria in the selection of the sample to be studied, and are presented below.

HOW MANY NEW IMMIGRANTS ARE THERE?

The actual facts revealed in Table 1, below, should be reassuring to those who have thought of hordes of refugees overrunning the country, even if they are at the same time disquieting to those who wait for rescue from the horrors of Nazism.

Table 1 was prepared to clarify the complicated and detailed immigration statistics that show the probable number of immigrants who might legitimately be considered in any kind of competition with Americans. When all who have come to the United States since 1933 are classified as immigrants or non-immigrants, the non-immigrant group accounts for almost two-thirds of the total -- 1,214,704.

On the theory that these persons are not legitimately chargeable to the refugee labor market, the figure of 818,988 non-immigrants -- (those entering as temporary visitors, in transit, students, or in accordance with trade agreements) -- for the years from 1933 through 1940 excludes those aliens who came into the United States as government officials or as returning residents.

---

* By special arrangement it was possible to copy from the records in the Washington, D.C., office of the Bureau data on various items not tabulated separately in the published tables.

TABLE 1

Aliens, Immigrants and Non-immigrants, Exclusive of Government Officials and Returning Residents Admitted to the United States, 1933-41

	Total	Period I							Period II	Period III	Period IV
		Total	1933	1934	1935	1936	1937	1938	1939	1940	1941
Total	1,214,704	821,134	84,190	104,590	123,623	138,404	174,136	196,191	218,350	175,220	151,784
Immigrants	395,716	241,962	23,068	29,470	34,956	36,329	50,244	67,895	82,998	70,756	51,776
Non-immigrants	818,988	579,172	61,122	75,120	88,667	102,075	123,892	128,296	135,352	104,464	100,008
Temporary visitors	544,607	390,973	36,899	49,833	61,633	73,313	89,455	79,840	88,309	65,325	
In transit	255,269	174,850	22,693	23,687	24,931	26,571	31,822	45,146	44,115	36,304	
Students	13,322	9,096	877	1,048	1,377	1,515	1,828	2,451	2,182	4,044	
Trades	5,790	4,253	653	552	726	676	787	859	746	791	

IMMIGRANT AND NON-IMMIGRANT

Very few of these non-immigrants enumerated above are
officially in the labor market. Obviously, the more than
a quarter of a million persons in transit to other countries are not working in America. Students, of whom there
were 13,322, must obtain special permission for work in
other than academic pursuits. Those here on trade agreements are carrying out the affairs of their foreign employers. Officially, none among the 544 thousand visitors
who have entered the country between 1933 and 1940 are
permitted to work unless it can be proven that their
skills are not replaceable.

From the point of view of competition with American
labor, a cumulative total of 395,716 is very small. The
above figures are not in comparison with those of aliens
returning to their countries in the past decade, in consequence leaving a net immigration below the quota allot-
ment.

QUOTA AND NON-QUOTA IMMIGRANTS

Of greater interest in connection with the present study
are the figures entitled immigrants, 447,492, for the
years from 1933 through 1941. This includes quota and non-
quota immigrants from all countries. In the aggregate the
total is less than half a million for the nine-year period.

The distinction between quota and non-quota immigrants
is made to separate two groups of immigrants, both intend-
ing to enter the United States for permanent residence.
Within the quota, which is annually allotted to each country, on the basis of ratios established a long time ago,
there is a preferred section to which the following
classes of immigrants are chargeable before other immigrants may apply for their quota numbers. First preference on the quota for each country is given to:

1. Parents of American citizens.
2. Husbands of American citizens, married to them after
   July 1, 1932.
3. Persons skilled in agriculture, their wives and their
   children under 18 years of age. (This category is
   not now being honored on the preference quota because there is no longer a shortage of agricultur-
   ists.)

Second preference on the quota is given to:
1. Wives and minor children of alien men legally in the
   United States.
2. The minor children, but not the husbands, of alien
   women legally in the United States.

Classes of immigrants labeled non-quota and therefore entitled to enter outside the quotas for their countries are:
1. The wives and children under 21 years of age of American citizens.
2. The husbands of American citizens who were married
   to them before July 1, 1932.
3. Ministers and college professors who have continuously practiced their calling for two years and more
   prior to their application for admission to the
   United States, their wives and unmarried children
   under 18, if they have a contract with a church or
   college to carry on their calling in the United
   States.

The distinctions made above between quota, first and
second preference quota, and non-quota immigrants will
probably suffice for the purposes of this discussion even
if they do not cover all the possibilities.

The numbers of quota and non-quota immigrants, like
those of the non-immigrants, have decreased annually since
1939. During the immigration year ending July 1, 1941,
less than 52,000 quota and non-quota immigrants were admitted to the United States from all countries of the
world.

"REFUGEE" IMMIGRANTS

Because immigration statistics do not distinguish the
category "refugee" from non-refugee, it is necessary to
estimate the number of immigrants in each year who might
be legitimately labeled as refugees. One handicap to an
easy estimate is the fact that the published tables relate the number of immigrants to the country of last
permanent residence, which does not always coincide with
the country of birth nor with the country to whose quota
the immigrant is charged. Many people, Jews and other
anti-Fascists, first sought refuge in Europe outside of
Germany and, later, outside of Austria and Italy. These
people are classified in several ways: as immigrants from

the country of last permanent residence; as coming from
their country of origin; as Hebrews; or as French, German,
Italians -- classifications labeled "race." While "race" in
the immigration statistics is related to the country of
origin, and to the country of last permanent residence,
no cross correlation on occupation, age, or race, can be
made from the published tabulations for the country of
last permanent residence.

The caption "Hebrew" is the designation of the person
himself to the immigration officials and so may not include some who would be considered "Hebrews" by others.
As an illustration of some of the complications, there is
the case of the young man born in Berlin of an Aryan
mother and a Jewish father, a citizen of Hungary. As an
immigrant, the young man who was brought up a Protestant
by his maternal grandmother, is charged to the German
quota on the basis of which he appears in the statistics
from Germany as his country of last permanent residence
but as a Hungarian citizen, and a non-Hebrew, as he choses
to define himself. The non-Aryan restrictions, however,
prevented him from making a living in Germany.

In the sections below the details for arriving at the
estimated number of refugees from each of the European
countries are given, although every effort is made to
make the figures more rather than less inclusive. The
total estimate is considerably below that currently used
by the National Refugee Service, whose estimate of
200,000 includes all "Hebrews" regardless of the country
from which they have emigrated since 1933.

"REFUGEES" FROM GERMANY

In the present study all immigrants from Germany between
the years of 1933 and 1941 are considered refugees. The
objection that not all immigrants coming from Germany in
those years should be counted among the refugees is met
as follows:

a. It is likely that persons classified as in professional occupations, in addition to those who left Germany
for reasons of conscience or conviction, are refugees,
otherwise they would have had no reason to leave the country.

b. Non-Aryans, those who were one-half or one-quarter

TABLE 2

Yearly Estimated Number of "Refugees," Classified by Country of Last Permanent Residence

	All Periods	Period I	1933	1934	1935	1936	1937	1938	Period II	Period III	Period IV
Total "refugees"..	140,211	47,032	1,919	4,392	5,201	6,346	10,895	18,279	40,943	37,555	14,681
Austria...........											
Belgium...........	4,284								442	1,713	c-x
Czechoslovakia....									2,896	1,074	314
Denmark...........											
France............	13,709								883	2,575	5,177[c]
Germany...........	106,017	46,952	1,919	4,392	5,201	6,346	10,895	18,199	33,515	21,520	4,030
Great Britain.....	8,836								737	4,099	4,000
Hungary...........	1,760									1,450	310
Italy.............	1,745							80	732	733	200[a]
Netherlands.......									822	2,097	c-x
Norway............	488									488	b
Poland............	1,153									702	451
Roumania..........	247									247	
Spain.............	516								257	259	b
Switzerland.......	1,456								659	598	199[d]

a. Approximation.
b. Not available.
c. Figure for second quarter missing.
d. For last half of year only.
x. See under France.

Source: Releases of the Department of Justice, Immigration and Naturalization Service, Washington, D. C.

Jewish, estimated at 600,000 in Germany in 1933, would, no doubt, be included in large numbers among the refugees, because of the restrictive laws.

c. There must have been some active opponents of Fascism other than Jews in all classes of the German population.

d. Since Hitler's policies discouraged immigration, only those persons forced to leave the country would be likely to do so, unless they were Hitler's emissaries -- the number of which is unknown.

The German total, therefore, of approximately 106,000 is an overestimate, rather than an underestimate of the number of refugees from that country and Austria since 1933.

ESTIMATED NUMBER OF ITALIAN REFUGEES

In the total of approximately 1,700 refugee immigrants from Italy are included only those Hebrews who gave Italy as their country of last permanent residence, and who emigrated after the initiation of the anti-Semitic laws in 1938. This number would include not only Italian-born Hebrews but those who had been born in other countries, specifically Germany, and had emigrated after 1933 and for whom Italy presented a possible haven from Hitler.

Non-Hebrews from Italy are not included; probably the vast majority of those who opposed Fascism left Italy long before Hitler came to power. In the last two decades there has been considerable immigration to the United States from Italy, but chiefly of the lower socio-economic groups in response to the demand for unskilled workers and depressed economic conditions in Italy. None of these people could legitimately be called "refugees."

ESTIMATED NUMBER OF CZECHOSLOVAKIAN REFUGEES

All immigrants giving Czechoslovakia as their country of last permanent residence since the beginning of the fiscal year 1939 are considered refugees. This number (4,284) includes not only the native Czechs who fled the Hitler régime, but those who had fled earlier from Hitler and immigrated to Czechoslovakia for sanctuary.

ESTIMATED NUMBER OF SPANISH REFUGEES

Beginning with the date of the end of the Civil War in
Spain, July, 1938, all persons giving Spain as their last
country of residence are considered refugees. This date
marks the beginning of the fiscal immigration year 1939.
The number (516) is probably an understatement of the
estimate for 1940.

ESTIMATED NUMBER OF REFUGEES FROM THE NETHERLANDS, FRANCE,
    AND BELGIUM

The figure 13,709 for France, Belgium and the Netherlands is the combined total because not all the data were
available separately.

Although the invasion of Belgium occurred in May, 1940,
and corresponds with the end of the immigration fiscal
year ending June 30, 1940, all immigrants from Belgium
for that year are considered refugees because of the numbers among them who had probably come from other countries
to Belgium for protection against Hitler, and who left
during those two months.

The refugee estimates for France and the Netherlands
after the immigration year 1940 include all immigrants;
for the year 1939 they include only Hebrew immigrants.

POLISH, NORWEGIAN, AND ROUMANIAN ESTIMATES

While the figures -- 1,153 from Poland, 488 from Norway,
and 247 from Roumania -- are not complete they do include
all figures available on immigrants from those countries
for the fiscal years 1940 and 1941.

BRITISH, SWISS, AND HUNGARIAN ESTIMATES

For each of these countries, the only immigrants who
are considered refugees are those classified as Hebrews
who gave these countries as the countries of last permanent residence. The estimates are 8,836 from Great
Britain, 1,760 from Hungary, and 1,456 from Switzerland.

WHAT PROPORTION OF REFUGEES COME FROM EACH COUNTRY?

The four periods into which Table 2 is divided indicate, artificially perhaps, points in the stream of immigration determined by the events abroad. Not until 1939
did immigrants fleeing from Hitler begin to come from

countries other than Germany in any considerable numbers.
Even in 1939, when immigrants from Italy, Spain, and
Czechoslovakia joined the enforced procession, those from
Germany accounted for almost nine out of every ten. By
1940, Belgium, France, the Netherlands and Norway began
to contribute to the stream, in very much smaller propor-
tions, however, than they had ever sent to the United
States before the beginning of the war.

THE TOTAL ESTIMATE OF REFUGEES

Since the figures in Table 2 are not complete nor ab-
solutely accurate, but based on assumptions noted above,
good practice would indicate that the numbers should be
presented in rounded figures. Because the figures for the
fiscal year 1941 are least complete and lack details for
some countries it is assumed that the number of refugees
is closer to 22,000 than it is to 14,681 -- the number in
Table 2.

In relation to any theory of the effect of immigration
on the economy of the United States, it is clear that the
number of refugees in relation to the total population of
the United States is so small as to be numerically negligible. Approximately one person labeled a refugee has
been admitted in each of the nine years since the beginning of Hitler's régime for each 8,000 persons in our
total population.

On the other hand, while the total number of refugees
is undeniably very small, their concentration in a very
small section of the country creates a mirage of considerable size. The facts given below should dispel this il-
lusion and confine the problem to the geographically
small section of the country where refugees concentrate.

WHERE HAVE REFUGEES SETTLED?

According to the immigration statistics, the country as
a whole (exclusive of the eastern seaboard, which attracts
about two-thirds of the newcomers) has received so small
a proportion of the total immigrant group that their f-
fect on the life or the economy of the people living west
of the Alleghanies is slight, if expressed only in numeri-
cal terms.

TABLE 3

Estimated Ratio of "Refugees" to Immigrants, 1933-40

	All Periods 1933-40	Period I	Period II	Period III	Period IV
Estimated number of immigrants	396,000	242,000	83,000	71,000	52,000
Estimated number of "refugees"	150,000	48,000	41,000	39,000	22,000
Ratio of "refugees" to immigrants	37.9	19.8	49.4	54.9	42.3

Based on the figures of the Alien Registration in December, 1940, New York State had a major proportion of all aliens. This number, of course, includes not only the new, but those old immigrants who have not yet become naturalized. The "old world flavor" of the population of New York State is attested by the fact that in 1930, seven out of every ten individuals in New York City were born abroad, or one or both of their parents were born abroad; while for the United States as a whole, this was true of about three out of every ten persons.

The figures below do not necessarily represent the actual present whereabouts of all the new immigrants because they are based on statements to the immigration official at the time of entry. The newcomer does not always know where he will settle permanently, nor how many shifts he, like those who came to this country in earlier decades, will have to make. The two seaboards, though in very different proportions, are the favored areas for settlement. Fewer than five out of every hundred immigrants to the United States in 1939 and 1940 reported that they planned to settle in Massachusetts, in New Jersey, or in Pennsylvania, respectively. Approximately nine out of every hundred gave California as their destination. On the basis of these figures it appears that facilitating the adjust-

TABLE 4

All Immigrants Admitted during Fiscal Years 1939 and 1940,
Classified by Intended Future Permanent Residence as
Reported to Immigration and Naturalization Service

Intended Future Permanent Residence	Fiscal Year 1939		Fiscal Year 1940	
	Number	Percent	Number	Percent
All Immigrants	82,998	100.0	70,756	100.0
New York State	42,637	51.4	36,494	51.7
California	6,427	7.7	5,714	8.1
Illinois	4,353	5.2	3,629	5.1
New Jersey	3,779	4.6	3,001	4.2
Michigan	3,461	4.2	3,190	4.5
Pennsylvania	3,384	4.1	2,641	3.7
Massachusetts	3,219	3.9	2,755	3.9
Ohio	2,163	2.6	1,773	2.5
Texas	2,027	2.4	1,421	2.0
Other States	11,548	13.9	10,138	14.3

ment of the immigrant after he arrives in the United
States is the task mainly of the eastern seaboard states
and, in particular, of New York State.

HOW OLD ARE THEY?

Because the very young, the old, and some women are not
in the labor market among any group of people, it is of
interest to examine the age distribution of the refugees.
Table 5, below, assembled from the data of the Department
of Immigration and Naturalization, on age at the time of
arrival, accounts for a total of 175,219 immigrants.*

---

* It will be noted that this total is approximately 2,000

It will be noted that the age classification for the period beginning July 1, 1939 is in twelve, rather than in six groups as it was before that period. This difference in method of classification makes exact comparisons on age distribution in the three immigration periods difficult. The proportions of those under twenty-one in Period I and Period II shows very little difference; 28.8 percent in the first case and 27.3 percent in the second. The main shift is noted in the proportion of refugees between the ages of twenty-two and twenty-nine years for twenty-five out of every hundred immigrant refugees in the first period in contrast to about sixteen out of every hundred coming to the United States in the second period. In the second period, 36.7 percent were over thirty-eight years of age; whereas in the first period, this age group accounted for 26.0 percent of the total. Obviously a larger proportion of older people were included in the second period's immigrant crop than in the earlier one. The figures for the third period accentuate the trend noticeable in the second towards increasing proportions of refugees over forty and decreasing proportions under sixteen years of age at the time of arrival. In each of the three periods, however, the proportion of refugees below sixteen and over forty-five accounts for at least 32 percent, indicating that three-tenths to four-tenths percent of the total refugee group are probably not at work.

These differences in the ratios of young to old in each of the four immigration periods are no doubt related to the occupational distribution of the refugees which, in turn, reflects changes in immigration policy of the United States as well as changing conditions abroad. Because it has been necessary since 1924 to secure an affidavit from a relative, the entrance of the recent immigrants into the United States has been determined largely by the character of the preceding immigration. For some of those who now seek admission from Hitler-dominated countries, conditions are unfavorable, because in the past immigrants from these

---

larger than that in the table on occupations reported at time of arrival. In the age classification the Dutch race included the Flemish, in the other classification the Dutch were separately classified.

TABLE 5

Refugee Immigrants, 1933-40, Classified by Age
at Admission, Each Period, Number and Percent

Age Group	Period I 1933-38 Number	Percent	Period II 1938-39 Number	Percent	Age Group	Period III 1939-40 Number	Percent
Refugee Immigrants	79,197	100.0	50,393	100.0		45,629	100.0
Under 16	12,900	16.3	8,356	16.6	Under 11	3,717	8.2
16 - 21	9,897	12.5	5,407	10.7	11 - 15	2,779	6.1
22 - 29	20,544	25.9	8,459	16.8	16 - 20	4,116	9.0
30 - 37	15,262	19.3	9,653	19.2	21 - 25	3,208	7.0
38 - 44	7,880	9.9	7,224	14.3	26 - 30	4,607	10.1
45 years and over	12,714	16.1	11,294	22.4	31 - 35	5,168	11.2
					36 - 40	5,063	11.1
					41 - 45	4,442	9.8
					46 - 50	3,724	8.2
					51 - 55	2,975	6.5
					56 - 60	2,306	5.1
					Over 60	3,524	7.7

countries came most frequently from the working class
groups. In Germany, at least, where class structure formerly was fairly permanent, members of the higher socio-
economic classes were unlikely to have well-to-do relatives in the United States to whom they could turn for
affidavits. The well-to-do could make provision at home
for the unadjusted and the discontented. Among the lower
socio-economic groups these persons like many other American immigrants were more apt to seek their fortune in a
new country.

It should not be assumed, however, that all those who
sought to come and who had relatives in America were

necessarily of a lower socio-economic group. The earliest
German immigration to this country, the result of a polit-
ical upheaval (1848) brought many members of the upper
socio-economic group to the United States, whose descendants no doubt have furnished German relatives with affidavits.

BUTCHERS, BAKERS, AND CANDLESTICK MAKERS

Table 6, below, reveals on the basis of statements made
to the immigration officials at the time of arrival in
the United States whether or not the immigrant was working in Europe.

The figure of 173,094 (approximately 2,000 less than
the total in the age distribution of refugee immigrants
[Table 5 above] and 20,000 more than the estimated total
number of refugees in Table 2) was obtained as follows:
The published tables use only half a dozen classifications,
not entirely comparable with the occupation and industry
classifications in current use by employment services,
guidance bureaus, or the Bureau of Alien Registration and
the Bureau of Labor Statistics. In order to break down
the classification "skilled" -- which in the published releases accounted for so large a proportion of the immigrant group -- it was necessary to retabulate from the
code sheets in the Washington office of the Bureau of Immigration and Naturalization the reported occupations by
"race" at time of arrival of:

   a. All the immigrants classified as Germans for each
      year, 1933-40.
   b. All immigrants classified as Hebrews for each year,
      1933-40.
   c. All Slovaks, including Czechs, for the years 1939
      and 1940.
   d. All Spaniards for the years 1939 and 1940.
   e. All Scandinavians for the year 1940.
   f. All Belgians for the years 1939 and 1940.
   g. All French, all Dutch, and all Poles for the year
      1940.

   Tables 6 and 7, below, classify the refugee immigrants
for whom the data were assembled according to the instruc-
tions above, and for each period except the last. It will
be noted that the percent of immigrants who had worked

TABLE 6

Refugee Immigrants Classified by Work Status in Europe,
Reported At Time of Arrival in United States, Each Period, Number and Percent

Work Status	Total 1933-40		Period I 1933-38		Period II 1938-39		Period III 1939-40		Period IV 1940-41	
	Number	Percent	Number	Percent	Number	Percent	Number	Percent	Number	Percent
Total Refugee Immigrants	173,094	100.0	78,932	100.0	49,165	100.0	44,997	100.0	*	
Formerly occupied	78,213	45.2	37,503	47.5	21,740	44.2	18,970	42.2	*	
Formerly not occupied	94,881	54.8	41,429	52.5	27,425	55.8	26,027	57.8	*	

* Figures are not available at present.

TABLE 7

Refugee Immigrants Reporting Former Occupation, 1933-40
Classified by Major Occupational Group, Number, and Percent

Former Occupation	Total 1933-40		Period I 1933-38		Period II 1938-39		Period III 1939-40	
	Number	Percent	Number	Percent	Number	Percent	Number	Percent
Total reporting occupation	78,213	100.0	37,503	100.0	21,740	100.0	18,970	100.0
Profession- and semi-profes-sional	16,616	21.2	6,939	18.5	4,981	23.0	4,696	24.8
Managerial and official	22,964	29.4	9,101	24.3	7,641	35.1	6,222	32.8
Clerical and sales	11,243	14.4	4,698	12.5	3,538	16.3	3,007	15.9
Service	8,063	10.3	5,272	14.1	1,813	8.4	978	5.1
Agriculture, fishery, and forestry	2,195	2.8	1,340	3.6	454	2.1	401	2.1
Skilled	13,126	16.8	7,348	19.6	2,878	13.2	2,900	15.3
Semi-skilled	680	0.8	275	0.7	47	0.2	358	1.9
Unskilled	1,081	1.4	582	1.5	205	0.9	294	1.5
Miscel-laneous	2,245	2.9	1,946	5.2	183	0.8	114	0.6

abroad increases from 52.5 percent for those coming before July 1, 1938 (the beginning of the second period) to
58 percent for those coming in the third period. The fact
that with each succeeding immigration period the proportion of non-workers increases is consistent with the
changing age composition noted in Table 5, above, which
credits a greater proportion of immigrants in each succeeding period to the age groups over 40. This should re-
assure those who think of the entire immigrant group as
in the labor market. The occupations those who formerly
worked followed is shown in Table 8.

Table 8 redistributes the 78,213 of the refugee immigrants who reported that they were working abroad, according to the major occupational group to which they would
be credited on the basis of their reported occupation in
Europe.

Whereas the official and managerial category, Table 8,
accounts for almost thirty, and the professions for
twenty-one out of every hundred who reported work in
Europe, these proportions change considerably in the succeeding periods. For example, the professionals rise from
18 percent of the total reported in the first period to
almost 25 percent in the third period. By 1940, the managerial and official classification accounted for thirty-
three out of every hundred; whereas in the first period
it represented twenty-four out of every hundred.

On the other hand, the proportion of agricultural workers varies only from 3.6 percent in the first period to
2.1 percent in the third period.

The percentage in the service occupations falls from 14
percent in the first period to 5 percent in the third.
The changes in these categories, however, do not affect
the major fact that the three categories -- professional,
managerial, and clerical and sales -- account for from
55.2 percent of the immigrants in the first period to
73.8 percent in the third. On the whole, this presents
little or no competition to the vast army of skilled,
semi-skilled, and unskilled workers in the United States,
even though they may, if concentrated in one city, make a
few professionals temporarily uncomfortable. Nor are the
total number of immigrants in the professional group when
distributed over nine years very alarming in a country
that is short of physicians.

TABLE 8

Refugee Immigrants Reporting Professional Occupation
in Europe, Classified by Period of Immigration

Professional and semi-professional occupations	Total 1933-40	Period I 1933-38	Period II 1938-39	Period III 1939-40
Total	16,616	6,939	4,981	4,696
Clergy	1,088	578	246	264
Physician	3,911	1,768	1,223	920
Dentist	148	--	--	148
Oculist	14	--	--	14
Nurse	291	--	--	291
Teacher	2,092	822	638	632
Professor	256	--	--	256
Literary and Scientific	1,196	612	438	146
Editor	172	47	34	91
Lawyer	1,346	413	484	449
Accountant	1,253	690	427	136
Engineer	1,334	515	391	428
Chemist	181	--	--	181
Actor	349	156	98	95
Sculptor, Artist	335	129	103	103
Photographer	333	115	117	101
Architect	244	82	91	71
Musician	823	316	278	229
Other	1,250	696	413	141

Source: Releases of Department of Justice, Bureau of Immigration and Naturalization.

Table 9 which distributes the 16,616 refugee immigrants who reported that they were pursuing professional occupations in Europe, shows interesting variations in the numbers in the various professions in each period.

In the total, the 3,911 physicians and the 2,348 teachers and professors considerably outnumber lawyers and engineers, each of which accounts for approximately 1,350 persons. Literary and scientific persons (1,196) outnumber the ministry with 1,088 followers.

In the third period, the number of physicians decreased to 920; approximately one-half the number (1768) who arrived in the fiscal year ending July, 1938. About as many teachers came over in the third period as arrived in the first. The number of scientific and literary persons dropped from 612 in period I to 146 in period III. The absolute number of lawyers, engineers, and musicians, remained fairly constant in all three periods, accounting for approximately 450, 400-500, and 300, respectively.

No doubt these differences in the number and proportion of professionals coming in the third period relate directly both to the increasing number of countries contributing to the refugee immigrant total in the three periods, as well as to the decision of members of certain professional groups to emigrate earlier than did others.

Table 9 gives in some detail the occupations for the 22,964 persons classified as managerial and official in the three periods. The number of manufacturers fluctuates from 267 to 363. The total number of bankers is small, not more than 134 individuals classified as bankers emigrated in any one of the three periods.

The category which accounts for nine-tenths of all immigrant refugees (21,509) is that of merchants and dealers. The size of this group is probably due to the fact that refugee immigrants are predominantly from large centers in which merchants and dealers account for a large proportion of all those gainfully employed. Many merchants and dealers would have liquid assets to facilitate their immigration, just as the stock in trade of professors, physicians, nurses, and musicians should theoretically enable them to make a living in countries other than their own. This is an advantage which refugee lawyers do not have.

The marked decrease in the number of servants from 4,963

TABLE 9

Refugee Immigrants Classified by Former Occupational Group
and by Period of Immigration

Former Occu- pational Classification	Total 1933-40	Period I 1933-38	Period II 1938-39	Period III 1939-40
Agricultural, Fishery and Forestry	2,195	1,340	454	401
Farmer	1,449	845	305	299
Farm Laborer	570	409	112	49
Fisherman	22	8	2	12
Gardener	154	78	35	41
Manufacturing and Official	22,964	9,101	7,641	6,222
Banker	393	134	126	133
Government Official	4	1	0	3
Manufacturer	960	267	330	363
Merchant and Dealer	21,509	8,648	7,176	5,685
Hotelkeeper	98	51	9	38
Service Occupa- tions	8,063	5,272	1,813	978
Servant	7,336	4,963	1,658	715
Housekeeper	178			178
Barber	549	309	155	85
Clerical and Sales	11,243	4,698	3,538	3,007
Clerk	7,342	3,427	2,093	1,822
Agent	3,901	1,271	1,445	1,185

Source: Releases of Department of Justice, Bureau of Immigration and Naturalization.

in the first period to 715 in the third period, relates
probably to the decrease in the excess of females over
males arriving in the first refugee immigrant group, since
families who came in the first period were in a better
position to bring over, or to send for, servants, than were
were those who came in the later periods, frequently after
transit in several countries.

The scarcity among immigrants of persons following such
pursuits as agriculture, fishery, and forestry is empha-
sized by the small total (2,195) which represents approximately one out of every 800 persons who emigrated.

Of greatest interest in connection with the current demand for skilled workers (see the details in Table 10) is
the total of 13,126 immigrants who since July, 1932, have
been classified under the general heading of skilled occupations. This category accounts for almost every sixth
person among the formerly employed refugee immigrants.

The textile and apparel industries account for the
largest number (4,254). Food (2,794), building and construction (1,862), the metal trades (1,600), rank second,
third, and fourth, respectively, in the numbers of skilled
immigrants. The percent of immigrants in textile and apparel industries increased in the second and third periods,
while the number in the metal trades and in construction
decreased in the last two periods.

SEX AND MARITAL STATUS

In the total immigrant group of 175,219, approximately
3,000 more women than men came over during the nine years
(Table 11). In the period ending July 1, 1939, 675 more
men than women emigrated. There has never been an abun-
dance of servants. Beard in his Rise of American Civili-
zation wrote of the lament of the colonial housewives on
the difficulty of securing competent servants.

The marital status of the immigrant group indicates very
small proportions of widowed (4.4 percent) and divorced
(1.2 percent) in each period (Table 11). Striking differences, however, are found in the percentage of single
persons, which decreased from 52 percent in the first
period to 39.5 percent in the third period. This was due,
no doubt, to the fact that in the first period it was
frequently the custom for the young people to precede

TABLE 10

Refugee Immigrants Reporting Skilled Occupations in Europe,
by Immigration Period

Skilled Occupations	Total 1933-40	Period I 1933-38	Period II 1938-39	Period III 1939-40
Total	13,126	7,348	2,878	2,900
Building and Construction	1,862	1,037	379	446
Painters	593	336	147	110
Carpenters	585	337	115	133
Locksmiths	328	225	63	40
Plumbers	107	43	27	37
Masons	87	57	16	14
Plasterers	10	8	1	1
Electricians*	82	--	--	82
Iron and Steel Workers	70	31	10	29
Metal Trades	1,600	907	387	306
Mechanics	847	461	198	188
Machinists	189	132	33	24
Engineers	252	120	60	72
Tool and Die Makers	201	125	71	5
Blacksmiths	63	43	13	7
Metal Workers	48	26	12	10
Lumber and Furniture	263	125	71	67
Cabinet Makers	107	55	25	27
Upholsterers	145	62	44	39
Sawyers	11	8	2	1
Textile and Apparel	4,254	1,952	1,193	1,109
Tailors	1,487	715	420	352
Dressmakers	1,111	476	333	302
Furriers	618	275	171	172
Shoemakers	428	236	98	94
Milliners	276	101	80	95
Hat and Cap Makers	74	25	32	17
Weavers and Spinners	119	59	23	37
Textile Workers	72	30	16	26
Tanners and Curriers	50	20	18	12
Saddlers	19	15	2	2
Food	2,794	1,793	583	418
Butchers	1,809	1,176	410	223
Bakers	880	546	152	182
Brewers	81	55	14	12
Millers	24	16	7	1
Printing Trades	306	116	99	91
Printers	265	95	92	78
Bookbinders	41	21	7	13
Extraction of Minerals	35	24	6	5
Miscellaneous	2,012	1,394	160	458
Jeweler	256	82	73	101
Watchmaker	249	109	80	60
Pattern Maker	14	2	2	10
Cigar Maker	11	7	1	3
Tobacco Maker	1	1	--	--
Other	1,481	1,193	4	284

* Formerly classified under engineers.

TABLE 11

Refugee Immigrants, 1933-40, Classified by Period of Arrival, by Sex,
and by Marital Status, Number and Percent

Refugee Immigrants	Total 1933-40		Period I 1933-38		Period II 1938-39		Period III 1939-40	
	Number	Percent	Number	Percent	Number	Percent	Number	Percent
Total	175,219		79,197		50,393		45,629	
Sex								
Male	85,686		38,039		25,534		22,113	
Female	89,533		41,158		24,859		23,516	
Marital Status								
Single	81,927	46.8	41,150	52.0	22,795	45.2	17,982	39.4
Married	83,490	47.6	33,777	42.6	24,810	49.2	24,903	54.6
Widowed	7,681	4.4	3,395	4.3	2,121	4.3	2,165	4.7
Divorced	2,121	1.2	875	1.1	667	1.3	579	1.3

Source: Releases of Department of Justice, Bureau of Immigration and Naturalization, Washington, D. C.

their parents, for whom they sent as soon as they were
established. Many parents found it easier to remain abroad
during the first period than did the children, who were
prevented from entering their chosen careers. The parents,
on the other hand, were permitted to continue in some
fashion in their old business, if they were merchants --
and more than half of them were -- until late in 1938 or
early in 1939.

SUMMARY

On the basis of the tables presented above the refugee
immigrant group is not larger than 150,000 if the non-
immigrant aliens who come on visitors' visas, in transit,
etc., are deducted from the total number of aliens entering the United States since July, 1932. These persons are
excluded because, with some exceptions not easy to track
down, there should be few competitors with Americans from
this group.

While probably at least half, 75,000, of these immigrant
refugees make their homes in New York State, the remainder
are fairly widely and sparsely scattered. A few cities in
California, Massachusetts, New Jersey, Pennsylvania, Illinois, Michigan, and Ohio provide homes for the majority of
those refugee immigrants who settle outside of New York
State. Relatively small proportions of them, on the basis
of reports to the immigration officials, settled in the
deep south or the northwest.

The countries of last permanent residence -- in some
cases, the country of origin -- from which the refugees
come are principally Germany, Austria, Italy, Czechoslovakia, Spain, Norway, and the Netherlands. Smaller numbers
have come from Roumania, Poland, Switzerland, and Portugal.
Because so many refugees hoped, at the first onset of
Nazism, to be able to return to Germany or Austria, they
did not immediately come to the United States. Not all of
them would have been able to come immediately, because of
immigration restrictions and difficulties in connection
with securing affidavits and visas. Before many were finally able to leave Europe they were classified as coming
not from their country of origin but from the country of
last permanent residence, which might have been any one of
the countries listed above. While Great Britain is not

under Hitler domination, it appears in the statistics because it served as the major transit country. In the final
analysis, however, there is no gainsaying the fact that
the majority of the refugees created by Hitler are of
German or Austria origin whatever their original country
of origin may have been.

Since the Nazi persecutions hit whole families and not
just individual members of a family unit, the present refugee group, in its very nature, represents a cross section
of the population of the countries of emigration. Former
emigrations to the United States were characterized largely by the excess of young men rather than family groups.
The Irish emigration in the 1850's and the Jewish emigration in the 1880's, both of which represented wholesale
exodus from the old country, were exceptions to this
general pattern.

Unlike the previous immigration, the present refugee
group has a smaller proportion of unskilled laborers and a
larger proportion of persons who had formerly been in the
professions or carried on successful business enterprises.
Rarely do people successful at home emigrate to a new
country unless they are forced to leave. Large numbers of
persons of Italian, Germany, and Irish stock in the United
States today, are the descendants of immigrants who when
they came to this country were unskilled or skilled workers. Their descendants are not to any great extent today
represented in the professional or managerial occupations,
such as those followed abroad by more than half of today's
refugees.

These facts have major psychological implications on the
ease or difficulty of the absorption of the new refugees
in the American scene and on their acceptance by their
immediate immigrant predecessors, many of whom had lower
socio-economic status in their own countries of origin.

II

REFUGEE ENTREPRENEURS

The data presented here are designed to show the nature
of refugee adjustment in terms of business enterprises.
The chapter concerns itself with the description of the
refugee entrepreneurs who were identified by a variety of
methods as carrying on business in New York City. Enterprise in this study is any concern which has a place of
business and employees. If the employees are only members
of the family the enterprise is separately classified and
the family workers are not included in the count of employees.

A refugee enterprise is one established by persons who
were compelled by the spread of Nazism to leave their
homes in Europe and to seek admission to the United States
as permanent residents. Those who have come on visitors'
visas, or in any of the other non-immigrant categories,
are not included in this count because they are theoretically not at liberty to engage in business enterprises in
the United States.

Consistent with the distribution of refugees in the
United States, which parallels that of the total foreign
white stock, New York State has by far the largest proportion of them.

Outside of New York State with its almost 52 percent,
the proportional distribution of immigrants, as indicated
in Table 4, ranked as follows: California, 8 percent;
New Jersey, 4 percent; Michigan, 4 percent; Pennsylvania,
4 percent; Massachusetts, 4 percent; Ohio, 2.5 percent;
Texas, 2 percent. All other states designated as the destination of immigrants in 1939 and 1940 accounted for less
than 14 percent of the total immigrant group in each year.

Thus, the major concern of this section of the study is
the analysis of data secured from more than 800 concerns
established since 1933 by refugees in New York City, the
center of commercial activity.

THE MASTER LIST

Since there is, unfortunately, no single source for enterprises classified according to whether or not the owner
is a citizen, the prospect list for this study had to be
built up.

The principal sources were: (1) notices of new enterprises in refugee newspapers; (2) articles in the refugee
press announcing the study and requesting information on
refugee enterprises; (3) interviews with consuls, bankers,
lawyers, insurance agents whose clientele was known to be
largely foreign; (4) concerns known to agencies and organizations with a refugee clientele; (5) suggestions from
key persons in trades and industries and department store
executives. Finally, many of the refugee owners who were
interviewed suggested other prospects.

Each new prospect was checked against the master list.
After three months new names turned up so infrequently that
it had to be assumed that the sources listed above had been
as fully tapped as possible. Attempts to extend the list
were unsuccessful even when a check was made against the
list of the Capital Loan Committee of the National Refugee
Service (see Appendix).

Forty small retail concerns were added, however, when
the names of owners appearing in the individual study*
were checked against the enterprise file. The fact that
these names did not appear in the retail list of refugee
enterprises suggests that this is a field which would need
to be separately and continuously canvassed because of the
nature of the businesses, which are so largely neighborhood affairs and are so frequently short-lived.

It is probable that the list is incomplete also for the
very large concerns in which the important participation
of refugee capital would not be public information. Some
of the earlier refugees and perhaps some of those who have
come over recently but have sojourned since 1933 in other
countries, were able to bring considerable capital. It is
generally known that some well-to-do refugees have invested their money in firms well established in America,
and some have become partners in American concerns. Some
may, like their American brothers, consider that business

---

* See Mimeographed Report.

investments are not at the present the most profitable
way of employing their capital. The size of these groups
cannot be estimated even through clues such as the con-
tributors' lists of various campaigns because again, like
some Americans, some refugees successfully avoid charita-
ble solicitation.

Although these groups may be of economic significance
and could be considered as contributing to the American
economic scene, none of them will appear in the study
since it is concerned with enterprises started by refugees, and not those into which refugees put money, no
matter how large a part of the business is so supported.

THE SCHEDULE

The initial interviews made it clear that various ap-
proaches were necessary to induce the owners of refugee
concerns to talk. A schedule was designed to minimize re-
sistance to certain types of questions (see Appendix).
Anonymity was assured by omitting names from the schedules and reserving them solely for purposes of identifi-
cation of duplicates in the file.

The pooled experience of staff members was studied by
the student interviewers before they went into the field.
In turn they were encouraged to report and discuss the
problems that they discovered. In some types of concerns
somewhat more persistence was needed and slightly more
address than the young student has ordinarily acquired.
In at least one-third of the enterprises the work of the
students was supplemented by experienced volunteer interviewers who were familiar with conditions in certain
industries.

Although the majority of the interviews were made by
personal calls at the place of business, it is of interest to note that trained workers were able to secure the
required data from approximately 200 concerns by judicious
use of the telephone. In some instances, the telephone
calls resulted in a request for a personal call or an official letter with a schedule.

Within three months the accumulated prospect list of
1,384 was canvassed. When the concerns no longer in business, and those incorrectly classified as refugee concerns, those who refused information plus those who did

not return the questionnaires were weeded out, there remained 829 refugee concerns in New York City for whom
schedules were filled out.

The reliability of the data, accepting limitations of
coverage mentioned above, is reasonably attested to by the
fact that the second sample -- 358 including the 200 interviewed by telephone and the 70 questionnaires returned
by mail -- yielded results so close to those obtained in
the first series of interviews that conclusions based on
that analysis alone would have been proportionately the
same in every respect. The additional canvass added only
to the total numbers in each category and did not disturb
the ratios or change the conclusions.

While the completed schedules offer many interesting
clues, this study is limited to the analysis of the data
which answer the original questions prompting the study.

CLASSIFICATION SYSTEM

The first problem, the knotty one of classification was
solved by using the 1929 industry classification of the
Census of Manufacturers; for wholesalers, the Census of
Business, 1935; for retailers, the classification of retail stores of the U.S. Bureau of the Census, 1935. In
the tables below, the enterprises are classified so that
they are comparable with the current American usage.

WHAT TYPES OF BUSINESSES DID THEY ESTABLISH?

Table 12, below, subdivides the enterprises into those
which furnish employment to members of the immediate
family and those which furnish employment to others. Of
the 820 concerns, only 114 fall into the first category
and, as would be anticipated, the majority are found in
retail trade (34) and service industries (22).

Concerns large enough to employ other than family members are most frequent under the caption "manufacturing,"
which accounts for 40.5 percent of all enterprises in
that category.

The four subdivisions of trade -- wholesale, retail, export and import, and service industries -- together make
up the next category and account for approximately half
of the total (351).

The negligible number of enterprises under "transport," "amusement," "mining" is consistent with the occupational classification of the refugee noted in the earlier section of this report.

From the figures below it is clear that the major business activities of the refugees are in the fields of retail trade and certain types of manufacturing.

HOW LONG DID IT TAKE THEM TO GET STARTED?

To the general question: "How long did it take the newcomer to get started in business?" Table 13 offers an answer. Until the year 1936 the number of enterprises established each year on the basis of the sample is almost negligible. Of the 68 enterprises established in that year, approximately one-fourth (26.5 percent) were established within the year of arrival in the United States. Within two-years almost half (46 percent) of these entrepreneurs had established themselves.

Those who came after 1936 were apparently able to start their concerns more quickly than those who came earlier, since the interval between the arrival and the establishment of the business decreases steadily for each period. For example, 68 percent of the arrivals in 1937, 75 percent of those in 1938 and almost 90 percent in 1939 reported that they were able to establish their businesses within two years.

As would be anticipated, the type of enterprise has some relation to the length of time necessary to establish it in the new country. Only a third of the manufacturers got their start in the year of arrival of the entrepreneur in the United States. Half of the wholesalers and half of the importers and exporters were established in the same year that the owner arrived in the United States. The fifty-two financiers took the shortest time to establish themselves in this country. In each group about two-thirds were established within two years. The longest time, probably because such factors as familiarity with neighborhoods and American methods play a greater rôle in successful retailing than they do in other types of business, was needed for the emigrating retailers to get started again.

TABLE 12

Refugee Enterprises Classified by Major Industrial Groups
and as Employing Family Members Only or Others
New York City, Summer, 1941

Industrial Groups	Total	Number of Enterprises Employing Family Members Only	Others	Number of Employees Other Than Family Members
All Groups	829	114	715	8,984
Finance	52	10	42	333
Manufacture	306	16	290	5,783
Trade	433	82	351	2,473
Wholesale	117	17	100	803
Retail	159	34	125	847
Export-Import	92	9	83	536
Service Industries	65	22	43	287
Other	38	6	32	395
Professional	27	6	21	110
Transport	8	--	8	250
Amusement	2	--	2	11
Mining	1	--	1	24

NEIGHBORHOOD DISTRIBUTION OF RETAILERS

Table 14, below, shows that of the 304 retail and service industries for which Manhattan addresses were given, almost half, ninety-six, were located in upper Manhattan, the section in which the refugees have most thickly settled. Only six shops were located in the Lower East Side, and only one in Harlem. Kips Bay, Yorkville, has a considerable number -- seventy. Fifty-two refugee shops were located in one health area (No. 48), which is bounded by Sixth and Third Avenues, 42nd and 63rd Streets, and is a main mid-town shopping center.

TABLE 13

Refugee Enterprises Classified by Year of Arrival of the Owner in the United States and by Year of Establishment of the Enterprise
New York City, Summer, 1941

Year of Arrival of Owner	Total Owners	Year of Establishment of Enterprise									
		1933	1934	1935	1936	1937	1938	1939	1940	1941	N. R.
All arrivals	829	5	6	15	25	52	144	249	234	65	34
1933	14	4	4	2	1	1	1	--	1	--	--
1934	16	--	2	5	1	3	2	1	2	--	--
1935	23	--	--	7	4	2	--	4	3	1	2
1936	68	--	--	--	18	13	19	6	7	3	2
1937	105	--	--	--	--	28	43	17	10	6	1
1938	217	--	--	--	--	--	73	88	39	9	8
1939	248	--	--	--	--	--	--	122	102	18	6
1940	83	--	--	--	--	--	--	--	63	18	2
1941	9	--	--	--	--	--	--	--	--	9	--
No Report	46	1	--	1	1	5	6	11	7	1	13

TABLE 14

Location in Health Center Districts and Health Areas in Manhattan
of 204 Retail and Service Industries
New York City, Summer, 1941

Manhattan Health Center Districts

Washington Heights		Riverside		Lower West Side		Central Harlem		East Harlem		Kips Bay, Yorkville		Lower East Side	
Health Area	Number of Enterprises	Health Area	Number of Enterprises	Health Area	Number of Enterprises	Health Area	Number of Enterprises	Health Area	Number of Enterprises	Health Area	Number of Enterprises	Health Area	Number of Enterprises
Total	49	Total	47	Total	31	Total	0	Total	1	Total	70	Total	6
1	3	11	--	39	2	8		17		36	4	53	3
2.10	4	14	1	45	--	10		20		37	2	58	1
2.20	6	18	1	46	1	12		21		38	--	59	--
3	12	23	3	47	4	13		22		41	4	60	--
4	10	27	1	51	--	15		25		42	1	62	--
5	7	31	21	52	14	16		26		43	--	63	--
6	5	32	3	55	--	19		28	1	44	--	65	--
7	--	34	13	56	--	24		29		48	52	66	--
9	2	35	1	57	7			30		49	3	67	--
		40	3	61	--			33		50	--	70	--
				64	--					54	4	71	--
				68	1							72	--
				69	--							73	--
				77	2							74	2
												75	--
												76	--
												78	--
												79	--
												80	--

DO THEY USE THEIR FORMER SKILLS?

With the generalization that the majority of these enterprises were established fairly soon after the arrival
of the entrepreneur in the United States goes an assumption of a carry-over of skills and, in some cases, a
carry-over of funds. Such a carry-over would be greater in
certain types of businesses than in others. For example,
of the forty-eight financiers for whom data were available,
thirty-one were engaged in financial operations abroad,
and nine were lawyers -- an occupation frequently associ-
ated with certain types of business activities.

Among 306 manufacturers (Table 15) 183, or more than
half, were manufacturers in the same line in Europe. Two-
thirds of those in the apparel and leather industries and
four-fifths of those in the diamond industry were formerly
in the same business. Forty-four others followed related
occupations such as manufacturing or were managers or owners of department stores.

Of the sixty-four who followed other occupations in
Europe (Table 16), one-fourth were skilled workers (nine-
teen), approximately one-eighth each were agents and lawyers, and fifteen had been engaged in other professions.

Thus, in the main these newcomers have transferred
their skills more or less directly to the United States
and without too great a loss of time.

WHAT ARE THE PRODUCTS?

In Table 17, below, manufacturers are classified according to the field of manufacturing and, if they reported a
new field, the nature of the process or product. They were
asked whether they had developed in America new patents,
new processes, or new products -- new in the sense that
they were not formerly known or made in America. Within
the limitations of inaccurate reporting or knowledge as
the extent to which some of these products may formerly
have been made in America or marketed here, the following
facts stand out:

(1) While there is considerable spread of activity in a
variety of fields covered by the twenty subdivisions of
manufacturers, the largest numbers of refugee manufacturers are found in apparel and textiles, food and beverages,

TABLE 15

Refugee Manufacturers by Industrial Classifications and
Their Former Occupations in Europe, Same Occupation,
Related Occupation, or Different Occupation
New York City, Summer, 1941

Industrial Classification	Total Entre- preneurs	Same Occupa- tion	Related Occupa- tion	Others	No Report
Total	306	183	44	64	15
Food and Beverages	38	19	4	14	1
Tobacco	--	--	--	--	--
Textiles	26	14	2	6	4
Apparel	73	51	9	11	2
Lumber	1	--	--	--	1
Furniture	7	5	1	--	1
Paper	3	2	1	--	--
Printing and Publishing	18	11	1	6	--
Chemicals	25	16	4	5	--
Petroleum and Coal	--	--	--	--	--
Rubber	1	--	1	--	--
Leather	35	24	4	6	1
Stone, Clay and Glass	3	1	2	--	--
Iron and Steel	4	--	2	2	--
Nonferrous Metals	21	17	3	--	1
Electrical Machinery	3	1	1	1	--
Machinery	7	3	1	2	1
Automobile Equipment	--	--	--	--	--
Transportation Equipment	--	--	--	--	--
Miscellaneous	41	19	8	11	3

TABLE 16

Refugee Entrepreneurs Classified by Industries and by Former Occupation
New York City, Summer, 1941

Present Industrial Classifications	Total Entre- preneurs	Merchants and Dealers	Professional			Managerial		Skilled Work	None	No Report
			Lawyer	Engineer	Other	Bankers and Agents	Managers			
All	306	216	11	4	15	10	4	19	12	15
Food and Beverages	38	25	2	1	5	2	--	--	2	1
Tobacco	2	--	2	--	--	--	--	--	--	--
Textiles	26	15	--	--	1	--	--	2	2	4
Apparel	70	53	--	--	2	--	3	8	2	2
Lumber	1	--	--	--	--	--	--	--	--	1
Furniture	7	6	--	--	--	--	--	--	--	--
Paper	3	3	--	--	--	--	--	--	--	--
Printing and Publishing	18	9	1	--	--	1	--	5	1	--
Chemicals	26	19	1	1	3	--	--	2	--	--
Petroleum and Coal	--	--	--	--	--	--	--	--	--	--
Rubber	1	1	--	--	--	--	--	--	--	--
Leather	35	27	1	--	--	3	1	1	1	1
Stone, Clay, and Glass	3	3	1	--	--	--	--	--	--	--
Iron and Steel	4	1	--	--	2	--	--	--	--	--
Nonferrous Metals	21	19	--	1	--	--	--	--	1	1
Electrical Machinery	4	2	--	--	--	1	--	1	--	--
Machinery	6	3	--	1	--	1	--	--	--	1
Automobile	--	--	--	--	--	--	--	--	--	--
Transportation Equipment	--	--	--	--	--	--	--	--	--	--
Miscellaneous	41	30	2	--	1	2	--	--	3	3

TABLE 17

Refugee Manufacturers Classified by Type of Manufacture,
the Nature of the Process, and as to Whether the Process
or Products Are New or Old
New York City, Summer, 1941

Manufacturers by Subdivisions	Total Enterprises	New			Old
		Product	Process	Patent	
Total	306	96	32	22	156
Food and Beverages	38	19	7	1	11
Tobacco	--	--	--	--	--
Textiles	26	6	3	--	17
Apparel	73	17	5	2	49
Lumber	1	1	--	--	--
Furniture	7	4	1	--	2
Paper	3	1	--	1	1
Printing and Publishing	18	2	1	--	15
Chemicals	25	7	5	5	8
Petroleum and Coal	--	--	--	--	--
Rubber	1	1	--	--	--
Leather	35	16	3	1	15
Stone, Clay, and Glass	3	2	--	--	1
Iron and Steel	4	2	--	1	1
Nonferrous Metals	21	2	2	2	15
Electrical Machinery	3	1	1	--	1
Machinery	7	1	--	4	2
Automobile Equipment	--	--	--	--	--
Transportation Equipment	--	--	--	--	--
Miscellaneous	41	14	4	5	18

leather and diamond industries (classified under nonferrous metals).

(2) About half, 149 out of 306, claim to have introduced
something new. Obvious illustrations are the special candies and cakes formerly obtainable in America only through
import, the many leather novelties previously coming
chiefly from Czechoslovakia, certain types of hand-made
knit goods, and special types of zippers and fasteners.
Less obvious are the results of the transfer of the diamond industry from Amsterdam to New York. This has resulted in the employment of engineers working on new
tools and cutters trained in processes new to America.

WHERE ARE THEIR MARKETS?

Two hundred refugee entrepreneurs engaged in some form
of foreign trade. Among these were eighty-seven manufacturers, of whom ten were making food and kindred products,
fifteen were in the clothing industry, twelve were in
leather, and seven in nonferrous metals. To these exporting manufacturers should be added the 113 exporters and
importers (Table 18) of whom the great majority (ninety)
were engaged in export, principally of general merchandise.

While there was considerable business with the Americas
-- twenty-four concerns exported to Canada, fourteen to
Central America -- the major business was with South
America; the market to which sixty-five manufacturers and
and fifty-one exporters send their goods, chiefly apparel,
leather, chemicals, diamonds, food, machinery, and general
merchandise.

Thirty-six refugee concerns report business with South
Africa, twenty with England, and thirteen with Australia,
which is of some significance perhaps in the development
of good relations between the hemispheres if the businesses are of sufficient size.

WHAT IS THE VOLUME OF BUSINESS?

The answer to this question was the most difficult to
obtain. Interviewers who understood the reluctance of newcomers did not press for detailed answers but were content
to get approximations in the form of percentage of raw
materials purchased in the United States and/or figures
on the volume of production or its dollar equivalent.

TABLE 18

Refugee Exporters and Wholesalers Classified by Industries
and as Exporting and Importing
New York City, Summer, 1941

Industry	Total	Export Only	Import Export	Import Only
All Classifications	113	74	16	23
Amusement and Sporting Goods	2	1	--	--
Automotive	--	--	--	--
Beer, Wine and Liquors	2	--	--	2
Chemicals and Paints	2	1	1	--
Clothing and Furnishings	8	8	--	--
Coal and Coke	--	--	--	--
Drugs, Full Line	1	1	--	--
Drugs and Drug Sundries	--	--	--	--
Dry Goods, Full Line	2	1	1	--
Dry Goods, Special Lines	5	2	2	1
Electrical Goods	--	--	--	--
Farm Products (Raw Materials)	7	4	--	3
Farm Products (Consumers' Goods)	1	--	--	1
Farm Supplies	--	--	--	--
Furniture and House Furnishings	1	1	--	--
General Merchandise	30	23	7	--
Groceries, Full Line	--	--	--	--
Groceries and Food Specialty Lines	5	2	--	3
Hardware	--	--	--	--
Jewelry and Optical Goods	8	3	--	5
Lumber and Construction Material	2	--	1	1
Machinery, Equipment and Supplies	5	4	1	--
Metals and Metal Work	8	6	2	--
Paper and Its Products	1	--	1	--
Petroleum and Its Products	1	1	--	--
Plumbing and Heating Equipment	--	--	--	--
Tobacco and Its Products	1	1	--	--
Waste Material (Iron and Steel Scrap)	2	2	--	--
All Other Products	19	13	--	6

TABLE 19

Refugee Manufacturing Enterprises Classified by Industries
and by the Approximate Percentage of Raw Materials
Purchased in the United States
New York City, Summer, 1941

Industries	All Manufac- turers	Percentage of Raw Materials Purchased in U.S.				
		1-25	26-50	51-75	76-100	Not Reported
Total	306	4	4	4	239	55
Food and Beverages	38	--	--	1	35	2
Tobacco	--	--	--	--	--	--
Textiles	26	2	--	--	18	6
Apparel	73	1	1	2	53	16
Lumber	1	--	--	--	--	1
Furniture	7	--	--	1	3	3
Paper	3	--	--	--	2	1
Printing and Publishing	18	--	--	--	15	3
Chemicals	25	--	1	--	21	3
Petroleum and Coal	--	--	--	--	--	--
Rubber	1	--	--	--	--	1
Leather	35	--	--	--	29	6
Stone, Clay and Glass	3	--	--	--	1	2
Iron and Steel	4	--	--	--	4	--
Nonferrous Metals	21	1	2	--	13	5
Electrical Machinery	3	--	--	--	3	--
Machinery	7	--	--	--	5	2
Automobile Equipment	--	--	--	--	--	--
Transportation Equipment	--	--	--	--	--	--
Miscellaneous	41	--	--	--	37	4

Table 19 based on the answers of those interviewed to
the question, "How much of your raw materials do you purchase in the United States?" shows that of the 251 out of
306 manufacturing enterprises for which information was
obtained, 239 reported the purchase of at least 75 percent of their material in this country. While no check
was possible on the accuracy of the statements, they furnish a general indication that these businesses are customers for American goods.

In Table 20, below, the approximate annual dollar volume
of the ninety-four manufacturers who were willing to report on this item totals more than eight and one-half million dollars.

More than a million dollars is reported by the clothing
industry and close to a million for the chemical and allied products. Granting that these figures may be over-
stated for the ninety-four concerns (which represent the
smaller enterprises in the main), if the figure of eight
and one-half million dollars is taken as approximately
one-third of the total business, the total amount would
reach considerable proportions. This is consistent with
the number of employees in this category.

NUMBER OF EMPLOYEES

In Table 21, below, the 829 enterprises are classified
as in Table 12 into two groups: Those employing only
family members and those employing others. The 715 enterprises in this second category are grouped according to
the industrial classification and number of employees.
While the caption "trade" with 351 enterprises outnumbers
that of manufacture with 290 concerns, the number of concerns with more than seven employees is almost twice as
large in the manufacturing category as it is in trade (174
in the former as against ninety-four in the latter). Nine-
teen of the manufacturers had over sixty employees each,
whereas only three of those in trade were in that group.

CLASSES OF EMPLOYEES

Table 22 distributes the figures for those manufacturing
concerns for which they were available, on the class of
employment offered; i.e., skilled, clerical, sales, etc.

As would be expected, while the majority of the employees are in the skilled and sales categories, it is

TABLE 20

Refugee Manufacturing Enterprises Classified by Industries
and by the Approximate Annual Dollar Volume Reported
New York City, Summer, 1941

Industries	Number of Enterprises	Number of Enterprises Dollar Volume Reported	Annual Dollar Volume
Total	306	94	$8,660,000
Food and Beverages	38	12	474,800
Tobacco	--	--	--
Textiles	26	9	592,510
Apparel	73	28	1,116,700
Lumber	1	--	--
Furniture	7	3	538,000
Paper	3	--	--
Printing and Publishing	18	5	126,000
Chemicals	25	8	947,000
Petroleum and Coal	--	--	--
Rubber	1	--	--
Leather	35	11	319,500
Stone, Clay and Glass	3	--	--
Iron and Steel	4	--	--
Nonferrous Metals	21	4	768,000
Electrical Machinery	3	--	--
Machinery	7	1	100,000
Automobile Equipment	--	--	--
Transportation Equipment	--	--	--
Miscellaneous	41	13	3,677,500

TABLE 21

Refugee Enterprises Classified by Major Industrial Groups, as Employing Family Members Only or Others, and by Number of Employees
New York City, Summer, 1941

Industrial Groups	Total	Number of Enterprises Employing Family Members Only	Others	1-3	4-6	7-9	10-12	13-15	16-30	31-60	61-120	121 and over
All Groups	829	114	715	276	141	81	65	22	74	33	16	7
Finance	52	10	42	18	8	3	5	1	6	1	—	—
Manufacture	306	16	290	60	56	41	29	15	46	24	13	6
Trade	433	82	351	182	75	34	26	6	17	8	3	—
Wholesale	117	17	100	50	23	6	9	2	7	1	2	—
Retail	159	34	125	71	21	12	10	3	3	4	1	—
Export-Import	92	9	83	36	24	12	5	—	3	3	—	—
Service Industries	65	22	43	25	7	4	2	1	4	—	—	—
Other	38	6	32	16	2	3	5	—	5	—	—	1
Professional	27	6	21	15	2	1	2	—	1	—	—	—
Transport	8	—	8	—	—	1	3	—	3	—	—	1
Amusement	2	—	2	1	—	1	—	—	—	—	—	—
Mining	1	—	1	—	—	—	—	—	1	—	—	—

TABLE 22

Employees of Refugee Manufacturing Enterprises, Classified by Industry,
in Which Others than the Owners are Employed, According to Types of Work
New York City, Summer, 1941

Industries	All Enterprises	All Employees	Professional	Executive	Sales	Clerical	Skilled	Unskilled	Domestic	N.R.
Total	306	5,783	262	128	761	389	3,243	996	4	--
Food and Beverages	38	433	5	5	153	21	170	79	--	--
Tobacco	--	--	--	--	--	--	--	--	--	--
Textiles	26	701	3	15	108	27	358	189	1	--
Apparel	73	1,479	1	12	106	51	1,110	198	1	--
Lumber	1	2	--	--	--	--	--	--	--	--
Furniture	7	265	3	4	10	7	225	16	--	--
Paper	3	124	8	--	2	13	93	8	--	--
Printing and Publishing	18	134	9	24	19	33	45	2	--	--
Chemicals	25	399	3	11	251	28	49	57	2	--
Petroleum and Coal	--	--	--	--	--	--	--	--	--	--
Rubber	1	16	--	--	--	6	10	--	--	--
Leather	35	593	--	14	45	27	416	91	--	--
Stone, Clay and Glass	3	24	--	1	--	--	23	--	--	--
Iron and Steel	4	14	--	--	1	1	12	--	--	--
Nonferrous Metals	21	553	3	8	17	61	305	159	--	--
Electrical Machinery	3	47	--	9	15	4	13	6	--	--
Automobile Equipment	7	365	181	4	1	45	127	7	--	--
Transportation Equipment	--	--	--	--	--	--	--	--	--	--
Miscellaneous	41	634	46	21	33	63	287	184	--	--

likely that some of those classified as salesmen are
peddlers working on a commission basis. The nature of
some of these enterprises lends itself readily to this
type of sales activity, one that appeals usually only to
people who are at a disadvantage in the labor market. It
is of interest to recall that the immigrant forerunners
of many of today's successful merchants began their careers with packs on their backs in the 1850's, and with
pushcarts in the 1880's.

AMERICAN AND EUROPEAN EMPLOYEES

The absolute figures on the number of employees by type
of enterprise and by nationality are given in Table 23.

The 714 enterprises out of the 829 which employ other
than family members account for a total of almost 9,000
employees (8,984). Almost two-thirds of these (5,783) are
engaged in manufacture, a figure twice as large as the
number in trade (2,473), the next largest category.

In the total, 5,919 or two-thirds of the employees are
reported to be Americans. The largest number are employed
in the manufacturing industries. On the other hand, trade
employs equal numbers of Europeans and Americans. In the
wholesale and in the service industries the Europeans outnumber the Americans, probably because of the nature of
the business.

FULL-TIME AND PART-TIME EMPLOYMENT

Among all employees similar proportions of Europeans
and Americans are employed full-time (approximately 75
percent of each). In finance, as would be expected, prac-
tically all the employees are on full-time. Only in the
category manufacture is there any considerable amount of
part-time or seasonal employment. For instance, one-fifth
of the Americans and one-seventh of the European workers
are seasonal.

PROPORTIONS OF EMPLOYEES IN VARIOUS MANUFACTURING GROUPS

According to Table 24 the largest number of manufacturing concerns make apparel. The seventy-three enterprises
so classified gave employment to the largest number of
individuals (1,543), of whom approximately four-fifths

TABLE 23

Refugee Enterprises Classified by Major Industries, Employing Other Than
Family Members, and by Number of Employees, American and European,
Full-time, Part-time, and Seasonal
New York City, Summer, 1941

Industrial Classifications	Employing Other than Family Members	Total Employees	Americans				Europeans			
			Total Americans	Full-time	Part-time	Seasonal	Total Europeans	Full-time	Part-time	Seasonal
Total	715	8,984	5,919	4,419	576	924	3,065	2,332	338	395
Finance	42	333	184	179	5	--	149	146	3	--
Manufacture	290	5,783	3,922	2,833	326	763	1,861	1,329	262	270
Trade	351	2,473	1,425	1,180	204	141	1,148	782	62	104
Wholesale	100	803	382	371	44	67	521	290	9	22
Retail	125	847	561	405	128	28	286	222	41	23
Export, Import	83	536	348	328	14	6	188	175	8	5
Service Industries	43	287	134	76	18	40	153	95	4	54
Other	32	395	288	227	41	20	107	75	11	21
Professional	21	110	55	38	7	10	55	29	6	20
Transport	8	250	101	159	32	10	49	43	5	1
Amusement	2	11	10	8	2	--	1	1	--	--
Mining	1	24	22	22	--	--	2	2	--	--

TABLE 24

Refugee Manufacturing Enterprises Employing Other Than Family Members, Classified by Number of Employees, American and European, Full-time, Part-time, and Seasonal New York City, Summer, 1941

Industries	Employing Other than Family Members	Total Employees	Americans				Europeans			
			Total Americans	Full-time	Part-time	Seasonal	Total Europeans	Full-time	Part-time	Seasonal
Total	290	5,783	3,922	2,833	326	763	1,861	1,329	262	270
Food and Beverages	36	433	267	166	65	36	166	116	20	30
Tobacco	--	--	--	--	--	--	--	--	--	--
Textiles	25	701	354	170	57	127	347	151	55	141
Apparel	69	1,479	1,090	607	112	371	389	279	88	22
Lumber	1	2	1	1	--	--	1	1	--	--
Furniture	7	265	256	254	--	2	9	9	--	--
Paper	3	124	106	106	--	--	18	18	--	--
Printing and Publishing	15	134	79	66	13	--	55	49	6	--
Chemicals	22	399	179	158	21	--	220	171	48	1
Petroleum and Coal	--	--	--	--	--	--	--	--	--	--
Rubber	1	16	11	11	--	--	5	5	--	--
Leather	35	593	284	239	18	27	309	274	11	24
Stone, Clay and Glass	3	24	21	21	--	--	3	3	--	--
Iron and Steel	4	14	4	3	1	--	10	9	1	--
Nonferrous Metals	20	553	469	348	13	108	84	70	13	1
Electrical Machinery	3	47	21	11	--	10	26	14	--	12
Machinery	6	365	344	344	--	--	21	21	--	--
Automobile	--	--	--	--	--	--	--	--	--	--
Transportation Equipment	--	--	--	--	--	--	--	--	--	--
Miscellaneous	40	634	436	328	26	82	198	139	20	39

are Americans. Twenty-five textile manufacturers employed
690 people, evenly divided between Americans and Europeans.

On the other hand, the firms manufacturing nonferrous
metals and their products report only eighty-three Europeans among the 552 employees. The six refugee concerns
engaged in the manufacture of machinery employed 344 Americans out of a total number of 365 employees.

Other concerns in which the proportion of Europeans to
Americans is very small are those which manufacture furni-
ture and lumber products, paper and allied products. In
the first group only nine out of the fifty-seven employees
were Europeans, and in the second, only seventeen out of
the 123 were identified as Europeans by the entrepreneurs.

SUMMARY

To recapitulate, for 829 New York City refugee enterprises, the tables above indicate little time lost in
establishment in the United States. More than one-half
were established within two years of the arrival of the
owner in this country. For those who came after 1936 the
interval between arrival and establishment decreased in
each year. The financiers were able more quickly to reëstablish themselves, and the retailers, as would be expected, needed the most time.

The majority of these enterprises are in manufacturing
and trade. Among the latter, a considerable proportion of
very small businesses give employment only to members of
the immediate families, chiefly neighborhood retail and
service concerns.

Among the 279 manufacturing concerns large enough to
employ other than family members, a considerable number
introduced products formerly obtainable in America only
through import. Many new skills have been taught to considerable numbers of American employees.

Almost 9,000 employees were accounted for on the pay-
rolls of the 715 concerns which employed other than family
members -- almost 6,000 were reported to be Americans.

Clearly the assumption that the refugee newcomer presents a considerable challenge to the economic security
of Americans is obviously an overstatement, if not a naïve
one. Some of the factors involved in an answer to the question whether newcomers do or do not displace Americans
will be briefly discussed at the conclusion of the study.

III

"CLOSE-UPS"

By Emmy Crisler Rado

From the schedules and the interviews with the entrepreneurs described in the preceding chapter were culled
the stories related below. They suggest new developments
in many fields and the consequent enrichment of America's
economic and cultural life.

MERCHANTS OF FINE LEATHER

Until recently, there was little work in fine leather
done in the United States. The Mark Cross Company, one of
the biggest leather houses, because of the difficulty of
securing an ample supply of skilled workmen, maintained
only a small American shop for repairs and a little special order work. The raw skins gathered from the four
corners of the world to make the fine leather goods sold
in the Fifth Avenue shops had formerly to be sent to Austria, Germany, Czechoslovakia, France, or England for proc-
essing and manufacturing. With the German invasion of Austria, the supply of goods to America was lessened, and
with the invasion of Czechoslovakia it all but disappeared.

Today, however, many of the experienced manufacturers
of fine leather goods and the skilled workmen who helped
them, have found a refuge in America. They have brought
their skill and their enterprise with them. American
leather merchants who previously had to send buyers to
Europe once or twice a year, now do not need to spend
this money abroad because they can supply their customers
locally. New York City's new leather industry makes every-
thing in fine leather from small lapel ornaments and bill-
folds to the finest of hand-made belts and gloves.

Among the enterprises in the New York study there were
thirty-five refugee leather manufacturers, twenty-four of
whom were in the same business abroad. These men gave employment to 577 persons, 303 of whom were refugees and
274 Americans.

There are not enough of these refugee workmen whose

skill has been handed down from generation to generation
to provide in America all the leather goods formerly made
abroad. Those workmen who have come have already taught
their skills to American workers. They have brought non-
competitive ability which they are sharing with their
American co-workers.

Some of the leather manufacturers complained that they
could not afford to put the same grade of material and the
amount of work into their products as they did abroad because of the high price of American labor. Other manufacturers, however, say that they can and are turning out
merchandise comparable in every way to the previously imported articles and at the same time adapt themselves to
American work conditions.

No doubt, a considerable part of this industry will continue to center in the United States even after the war.
The new immigrant has brought skills, machinery, and
tastes that will endure. Previously, a piece of leather
could not be sold as first class merchandise unless it
was marked "Made in England" or "Made in Austria." If the
present rate of reëducation continues, consumer preju-
dice against American-made leather goods will entirely
disappear.

Figures on the curtailed American import of gloves
alone show the possibility for expansion of American
business in glove-making. In 1937 the United States imported more than ten million dollars' worth of gloves. In
1940 glove imports from Belgium, Holland, France, and
other countries had dropped to less than two and one-
half million dollars. In 1941 some of these countries no
longer exported gloves. Clearly an enormous market for
gloves made in America is in sight.

The enterprise schedules showed glove establishments of
all sizes, employing from one to 140 workers. Many glove
makers are reported to have settled also in Chicago and
on the west coast.

ACRES OF DIAMONDS

During World War I a few diamond makers fled from Belgium to the United States and formed the nucleus of the
small diamond industry in this country. Since September,

1939, the diamond industry has grown so large that it
bids fair to rival the diamond cutting and selling industry of the Low Countries, which played an important part
in the economy of these countries. Many Dutch and Belgian
diamond merchants were fortunate in being able to escape
the Nazi occupation with their stock of diamonds intact.
By August, 1941, a considerable number of merchants had
established themselves in New York City. Firms which previously had only branch offices in New York now made the
New York office the headquarters for the firm and greatly
increased their activities in the United States.

The immigration of these diamond merchants had been
beneficial to the United States in more than one way. On
the wealth that they brought with them in its easily
portable form, they paid large duties. At the same time,
they prevented the Nazis from using the diamonds not only
for exchange purposes but for industrial purposes. They
introduced diamond working machinery to the United States
and had it copied here.

One diamond merchant has set to work a number of unemployed engineers to copy a diamond cutting device which
he has brought to the United States. In previously unoc-
cupied loft buildings, these diamond merchants have given
employment to office workers and to skilled artisans,
some of whom have come here from Europe within the last
three years. Some of these were diamond workers abroad,
others are being trained here for the work. One merchant
employs fifty American girls in his factory although
girls have never done this particular kind of work before.
There is nothing inappropriate about it since it is light,
clean work, and does not require any great amount of
mechanical skill.

At first, the diamond workers' union objected strenuous-
ly to the newcomers and opposed both further immigration
and any training program. However, with the growth of the
industry the American Federation of Labor has finally
agreed to the establishment of an apprentice system.
Young boys out of high school are taught to saw, cut and
polish diamonds. During a three-year training period they
are paid an agreed wage which is less than the minimum
established by the union for regular workers. One induce-
ment to undertake this long period of training is the

extremely high wage earned by experienced workers. While
the minimum is $100 a week, the modal wage during the last
year was nearer $350 a week. So great indeed has been the
demand and the reward for skill that some diamond merchants who had been cutters in their early days have gone
back to their trade which is more remunerative than their
business in many cases.

A plan to cut diamond "melee" or stones of a tenth of a
karat or less, used to decorate rings and other jewelry,
has resulted in setting up an enterprise which is the
first of its kind in this country. More than fifty refugee workmen and their apprentices are cutting these tiny
stones and the proprietor has plans to expand his plant.
Highly specialized machinery makes low production costs
compatible with the payment of standard American wages.

Although under changed world conditions some of these
diamond merchants will return to Europe, many will un-
doubtedly remain in the United States. One evidence of
the probable stability of this industry is the recent
purchase of a Seventh Avenue building by the newly-
founded Diamond Merchants Club. This club acts as an exchange similar to those formerly maintained in Antwerp
and Brussels.

REMODELERS OF REAL ESTATE

Real estate is another field in which America has bene-
fited by refugee enterprise. Not only have many vacant
offices been leased by manufacturers but money has been
invested in real estate. One diamond dealer is building
fifty houses on Long Island.

In 1938 some refugee architects persuaded some inves-
tors to buy houses that were run-down. The improvements
resulted in the converting of the old places into easily
rented inexpensive attractive small apartments. Money in
considerable amounts has been supplied by the nationals
from many different countries for real estate equities,
for building apartment houses, and even for low-cost
housing projects. Some of these operations are conducted
by individuals. Others are under the auspices of large-
scale investment concerns. At the other end of the economic scale is:

"THE FULLER BRUSH MAN"

Many people have felt that the refugee canvasser presents a persistent and annoying phenomenon. If he is a
problem, it is one that will solve itself.

It is natural that those who were formerly salesmen and
small manufacturers in their home countries and who come
here without funds, should fall back on peddling when they
first arrive. They scarcely know what else to do. Numerous
newspaper advertisements lure them with tales of fabulous
success. Like their American competitors they try their
hands and feet at the canvassing game. They too, fall by
the wayside, but only after they have found other oppor-
tunities for making a living.

Sometimes the energy and the initiative of one of them
organizes a central agency through which others work as
salesmen. One recent refugee now the head of a food products corporation has set up many peddlers in business. He
supplies them with the products at prices that do not
undercut comparable articles. They sell merchandise not
available in the stores. Their calls are regular and
their deliveries prompt. Some of these agents are now in
similar small enterprises of their own and in turn they
outfit the new peddlers.

These traveling salesmen help to establish markets for
various products not formerly purchased in any quantity
or easily obtainable. Having acquired a taste for them,
the home purchasers ask for them in the stores in which
they customarily market and, in turn, the distributors
are able to place their goods in stores that formerly
would not consider them.

In Philadelphia, a philanthropic loan society helps
peddlers establish themselves with the small sums of
money needed to buy stands in an open market in the poorer
section of the city. After a time some of the peddlers are
able to rent a store, just behind their stands. When members of the family work with the father they are able to
run both the stand and the adjacent store. Eventually, if
these undertakings are successful, the refugee saves
enough money to establish himself in a store in a more
prosperous neighborhood.

Working out from Philadelphia, there is a group called
"customers' peddlers." These men go to outlying factories

and villages to sell low-priced goods on the installment
plan. These peddlers are hailed as a blessing among the
clientele they visit, because many of these people have
no credit elsewhere, nor do they have time to visit urban
shopping centers.

Peddlers, in general, are stocked by other manufacturers
in much the same way as they are by the food products company referred to above. They carry gloves, artificial
flowers, cosmetics, hosiery, aprons, closet accessories,
etc. Eventually, the successful individual peddler is
metamorphosed into the salesman in an organized business.

CATERERS TO THE APPETITE

One branch of manufacturing into which many of the refugees have gone is foodstuffs. Refugee firms produce a
variety of products: sausages, wafers, candies made by
Austrians, Belgians, Czechoslovakians, French, and Germans - specialties of their old homelands. There was the
former journalist from Czechoslovakia who brought with
him a recipe for making oblaten -- a thin, sweet wafer,
until recently made only in Carlsbad. This product has
become so popular that the manufacturer is unable to fill
all his orders. His machinery and equipment now turn out
13,000 tins of oblaten a year, worth approximately
$20,000. With orders for almost twice that amount he is
arranging for the construction of new machinery which
will cost $4,000, and for the expansion of his present
staff of seven people.

Then there are the firms which make lebkuchen, formerly
available only on import from Nuremberg. Another refugee
firm makes all sorts of specialties formerly imported for
the baking trade. This firm employs seven people, pays
for $40,000 worth of advertising a year of its prepared
flour for rye and pumpernickel bread.

A former commercial chemist from Germany who spent a
year and a half in Scotland before coming to this country,
acquired a recipe there for orange marmalade which he is
now manufacturing in the United States. Although it is
made of 100 percent pure fruit and sugar, he maintains
that he can sell it for less than the other "pure" marma-
lades now on the American market.

A man and his wife employed five people in the manufac-

ture of kosher smoked beef prepared in accordance with
the Jewish dietary laws and never before available in
America. Another man, a former importer, has been able
to produce canned cauliflower good enough to bear Macy's
"Lily White" label, as well as that of S.S. Pierce.
Cauliflower has been considered heretofore almost impos-
sible to can.

Before they left their homeland, some immigrants
learned secret recipes from their friends. One Boston
couple now make burnt almonds, a south German specialty.
A man in California makes "Swiss chocolates"; a woman
makes raspberry syrup, a drink without which no child
who grew up in Central Europe could be happy. Another
woman is making a famous cheese spread, formerly fabri-
cated only in Holland from combinations of Dutch and
Swiss cheeses. Until recently all of these products were
available here as imports only. Some of them were not
even known.

Vermouth is being manufactured in America by the son
of a family that made vermouth in Italy for many genera-
tions. In the past, 90 percent of the vermouth used in
this country was imported. This now thoroughly acceptable
Italian type vermouth produced in America will probably
supply the American market. Herbs which formerly had to
be imported for the vermouth are now also being raised
in this country.

THOSE WITH AN EYE TO FOREIGN MARKETS

Dutch and Belgian importers living in America today
have brought their customer lists and their markets with
them. Exports which they made formerly from Belgium and
Holland to Africa and the Far East now go from America
to these countries. The number of licenses obtained
through the Belgian and Dutch Consulates indicate the
large volume of this export business. Some of this volume helps to make up partly for America's loss of many
of her former European markets. One refugee export business is now supplying five and ten cent stores established by other refugees in Colombia, South America.

A Dutch exporter of general merchandise came to New
York in 1939 to set up an American branch office for his
concern. He remained here long enough to establish it.

When, in the spring of 1940, he was about to return to
Holland, the Low Countries were invaded. Word from a
friend finally reached him that his entire business in
Holland had been confiscated. He determined to set himself up permanently in New York. Here he has opened tre-
mendous Far Eastern markets for many American manufacturers who have never bothered about exporting before.
A trip to the Congo and to East Africa will, he believes,
open still other markets in Africa and Asia with many un-
exploited possibilities for American exporters.

Apart from the larger European industries which moved
to this country during the past few years there are
several enterprises new to this country, distinctly use-
ful, and ordinarily not directly competitive with previously established American business.

ADVENTURERS IN PLASTICS

One firm makes a new type of portable engraving machine
for use on plastics, wood, metal, or any other substance
for while-you-wait monogramming in stores or factories.
This firm not only makes the machinery but rents it with
the services of a trained operator.

Another man manufactures a texture finish for use on
picture frames and other ornamented wooden surfaces. The
use of this finish eliminates at least four operations
which were previously necessary. It is now used not only
in factories but is sold in large quantities in art-
supply stores. It is so popular that several imitations
are now on the market.

A firm has patented a plastic zipper which is so fine
and so flexible that it can be tied in a bow like a piece
of ribbon. Fifteen engineers are working on the machinery
to manufacture this zipper and the company expects to
provide employment to hundreds of workers.

One of the former most famous European ceramic factories
is now established in New Jersey. This factory is run by
a family who have been potters since the seventeenth cen-
tury. They are employing American artists to create de-
signs which will meet the American taste demands.

MISCELLANY

A double top desk for use in offices is now being manufactured by a fairly large concern. The principle is an
adaptation of the roll-top desk which permits the user to
pull out a second top when a visitor comes into his office
and thus inconspicuously to cover up private papers. A
perfectly flat and convenient work surface is thereby
made available.

Another firm makes fine boxes for perfumes and cosmetics, which American cosmetic manufacturers formerly purchased in Europe. Now they are designed, printed, and
assembled in America, using a printing process previously
unknown here. Employment is given to skilled workers on
the machine and to artists in the designing room.

Still another refugee concern has developed a process
for carbonizing paper which will replace the use of ordi-
nary carbon paper.

Five highly skilled workers from Solingen, Germany, are
employed in a concern which sharpens knives and tools
used by doctors and dentists. Chromium plating and silver-
refinishing are also done in this plant.

A synthetic wax to replace a fine wax manufactured in
Poland, and which is no longer obtainable, is now manufac-
tured in a plant vacated by the Standard Oil Company.
The new company employs thirty-two persons, many of whom
have been out of work in the community since the Standard
Oil Company shut down the plant.

Another man who makes fuel oil emulsifier and sludge re-
mover has purchased a bankrupt company and hired almost
all of its former employees to produce products which
have never been manufactured in America.

MEN WITH PATENTS

The schedules told the story of the chemists and engineers who have brought patents to this country and who
have been taken over by large industrial organizations.
These organizations cannot, of course, be termed refugee
enterprises However, the work and the skill of the in-
ventors of the patents adds to the success of the com-
panies and provides employment for others. These men are
not competitors since the work that they do at present is
work which others in America do not know how to do.

STIMULUS TO NEW YORK AS AN ART CENTER

One of the most interesting cultural contributions of refugees to America's business has been the opening up of new art galleries. Although Paris used to be the world center for modern art only a relatively small percentage of the art products that Paris bought and sold were made by Frenchmen. The new art capital is Manhattan.

A number of art dealers from European countries have now settled in New York and have brought with them many pictures and plastics, among them some which did not meet Hitler's approval. These galleries are not considered competitive by those long established here, but are believed to stimulate business. In the opinion of the Director of the Museum of Modern Art, the one good thing about the exile to America of these fine works of art is their enrichment of a world where cultural freedom still exists.

To quote President Roosevelt's speech on the occasion of the opening of the new building of the Museum of Modern Art in New York City:

> The fine arts cannot thrive except where men are free to be themselves and to be in charge of the discipline of their own energies and ardors. The conditions for democracy and for art are one and the same. What we call liberty in politics results in freedom in art.

IV

RECAPITULATION, FINDINGS, CONCLUSIONS

This study has turned the lens on such aspects of the refugee problems as to its size and its distribution in the various sections of the United States. Because the available official statistics do not make it possible to distinguish the refugee from the non-refugee, it has been necessary to estimate the number, the family characteristics, and the occupational distribution of refugees, defining the immigrant refugee as a person who has come to America with the intention of settling here, in flight from Germany or any Hitler-dominated country since 1933.

Because the focus of the study was chiefly on the possible competitive aspects of the refugee problem, immigrant refugees have been distinguished from non-immigrant refugees. People here on visitors' visas, in transit to another country, as students, or because of trade agreements are not officially in the labor market and are therefore not included in the estimate. It has been shown that, with the exclusion of this group, there are approximately 150,000 immigrant refugees who came to America between 1933 and 1941.

It is estimated that 75 percent of America's immigrant refugees came from Germany and Austria, even though many of them have sojourned in Italy, Czechoslovakia, France, Belgium, England, Spain, or Switzerland before finally reaching America. The other 25 percent came from the countries listed above.

It is probable that California has attracted less than one in eight of the 150,000 refugee immigrants. Less than one in twenty each are in the states of Illinois, New Jersey, Michigan, and Pennsylvania. Fewer than one in twenty-five are in Massachusetts. Refugees are more likely to be found in urban centers. The majority of the affiants live in urban centers, since as a group their background is so largely urban as is the background of the majority of the refugees, and since the urban possibilities for making a living are greater.

As a consequence, the immigrant refugee is largely the

concern of New York State in which about half of the total
number have settled. There is at present no way of knowing
exactly how these 75,000 individuals are distributed in
New York State. On the basis of an estimate of the numbers
who have left New York to settle in other cities of the
state, it is assumed that there are approximately 65,000
refugees in New York City.

When the Alien Registration Division has time to sort
refugee aliens from other aliens in their files according
to date of arrival; i.e., since 1933, for country of origin (Germany, Austria, Czechoslovakia, etc.), for the
appropriate years, by present residence, by occupation,
etc., more exact figures will be available on the numbers
of refugees in each state and each city.

On the basis of the present study there appears to be a
maximum of 35,000 wage earners added by refugees to an
estimated total of 3,500,000 wage earners in New York
City, or a total addition of only 1 percent over a period
of eight years in this area of concentration. In the country as a whole, they have added but 82,000 workers to the
approximate 33,000,000 persons in the labor force in
cities of 100,000 or over, in the nation as a whole.*

Assuming that the characteristics of all immigrants
from the countries dominated by Hitler since 1933 apply
to the refugee group, the present refugee immigrant is
unlike earlier immigrant groups in that there is a fairly
even distribution of the sexes, a larger proportion of
persons over forty-five years of age, and a larger proportion of married persons and consequently, of family
groups. There is also a larger representation of persons
from the professional and managerial occupations than was
the case among immigrants from 1890-1932. Many of these
earlier immigrants had limited free educational opportu-
nities in their homeland and, in many cases, came largely
from the underprivileged of the country from which they
came.

If the characteristics of 65,000 immigrant refugees in

---

* Preliminary figures on employment status of persons
fourteen years and over in cities of 100,000 inhabitants
or more -- March 24-30, 1940. U. S. Bureau of the Census,
Washington, D. C., Series P4, No. 7, Table 2.

New York City are similar to those of the interviewed refugee group,* with the qualification that the findings are not absolute but have probable application, then the characteristics of refugee immigrants in New York City may be described in the following terms:

FAMILY SETTING

If the refugee families are of the same size and composition as those in the interviewed group, they should be approximately distributed in 25,000 households, as follows:

   a. One out of four in single person households.

   b. Three out of four are families with two or more members, in the majority of which both parents reside in the household.

   c. Approximately one out of eight families had no children.

   d. Approximately one out of four families have only children under 21 years of age.

COUNTRY OF ORIGIN OF FAMILY HEAD

   a. Three out of five of the family heads were born in Germany.

   b. One out of four was born in Austria.

   c. One out of twenty was born in Czechoslovakia.

   d. One out of twenty-five was born in Poland.

   e. One out of thirty-five was born in Italy.

   f. One out of sixty-five was born in Belgium and Holland.

   g. One out of a hundred was born in France.

FORMER OCCUPATION OF INDIVIDUAL

Based on statements of 43 percent of the sample interviewed, the 28,000 who were formerly occupied are distributed as follows:

   a. One out of three, or approximately 9,000 refugees were formerly in the professional or semi-professional groups.

---

* For details on method of selection and for tables, send for multigraphed report available for distribution through Social Science Department, Columbia University.

b. Almost one out of three, or approximately 9,000, were formerly in the managerial or official group.

c. One out of five, or approximately 5,600, were formerly in clerical and sales occupations.

d. One out of seven, or approximately 4,000, were formerly in skilled trades.

e. One out of ninety, or approximately 300, were formerly in service occupations.

f. The other categories, semi-skilled, unskilled, agriculture, fishery, and forestry, were not represented in this immigrant group.

ON PRESENT OCCUPATION

Many people who did not work in their homelands are now working either because they are now old enough to work or because their efforts are necessary to sustain their families. In some instances, women who did not work formerly are working now because there are jobs available for them, but not for their husbands.

a. Approximately one out of every six, or a few less than 6,000, immigrants in New York City are now in professional or semi-professional occupations.

b. One out of thirteen, or approximately 2,700, would be classified as a manager or an independent entrepreneur.

c. Approximately one out of four, or 9,000, are now clerks or salesmen. Among them are many former business men.

d. One out of three, or approximately 10,500, are working in skilled or semi-skilled occupations. They are employed largely in apparel, in food, in leather, and in jewelry manufacturing. Very few of them are in the building construction or metal trades.

e. One out of seventeen, or approximately 2,000, are now unskilled workers.

f. One out of eight, or approximately 4,500, are now in service occupations. Among them are many former housewives, not formerly working, and some former independent business men who reported that they had their own shops or businesses of their own.

PROPORTIONAL DISTRIBUTION IN COMPARISON WITH TOTAL WORK-
    ING POPULATION

A comparison with the usual distribution of occupational groups in New York City is not possible except for the
categories of professional, semi-professional, clerical,
and domestic service.

a. Whereas in 1930 professional and semi-professional
    occupations accounted for one in twelve of the
    working population of the city, among the refugees
    it accounts for one in six, or twice the proportion.
b. Clerical occupations accounted for approximately one
    out of six in the 1930 Census but one out of four
    in the immigrant refugee group.
c. Domestic service accounted for one out of seven in
    the 1930 Census and one out of eight in the refugee
    immigrant sample.

PREVIOUS AND PRESENT OCCUPATIONAL CLASSIFICATIONS COMPARED

Not all of those who worked formerly and are still working are classified in the same occupational group. The
shifts from previous occupational groups are indicated
below. Naturally, they are greater for some categories
than for others, since certain skills are more directly
transferable to a new country than are others. For example, some professional skills such as teaching, archi-
tecture, engineering are more easily marketed than are
the skills of the former business owners or managers. In
varying degrees the present occupations represent a lower
socio-economic status than that formerly claimed by many.
For instance:

a. Among the former professionals fewer than one out of
    two are now in the same classification.
b. Among the former managers less than one out of six
    are still in that category.
c. Among the former skilled workers seven out of ten
    are still in skilled occupations.
d. Among the former clerks and salesmen one out of two
    have remained in that category.

ON ECONOMIC STATUS

Approximately 87 percent of the interviewed families
reported the earnings of the working members of the

families (see Table 25). While these items were much less completely reported than others, they support the inferences below on the average amounts which the different occupational groups within the refugee group earned. In round figures:

a. The average salary of the employed refugee is less than $19 a week.

b. Among the professionals the average weekly salary is approximately $23 a week.

c. Among the managerial group the weekly earnings are slightly less than $25 a week.

d. Among the skilled workers they are just below $20 a week.

e. Among the unskilled, just less than $16 a week.

f. Among the workers in service occupations it is a little less than $15 a week.

g. One out of twenty who reported earned less than $8 a week, and fewer than one in 300 reported more than $110 a week.

On the whole these figures indicate the very modest earnings of the employed refugees. Data on the number of persons working per family support the inference that the individual's earnings are small.

Chapter III shifts the discussion to the subject of the actual business enterprises established by refugees in New York City. Through every possible resource 829 concerns established by refugees in New York City were visited and interviewed. That number excludes a few refugee concerns who did not wish to coöperate and those concerns in which the participation of refugee capital may have been important but not identifiable. The total is short with regard to the considerable number of one-man-retail-neighborhood business undertakings, frequently the first step in the establishment of the newcomer after he has graduated from peddling. It is probably also short in the number of enterprises which do not come within the definition of the study but which are undertakings of individuals who employ a half dozen or so "homeworkers" making gloves, novelties, or sweaters.

To the extent to which the facts revealed in the study are typical, there would appear to be among the refugees in business some such distribution as follows:

TABLE

Working Refugees Classified
and by Reported Weekly
New York City

Major Occupational Groups	Total	Total Reporting		Under $8		8-9.99		10-11.99		12-13.99		14-17.99		18-21.99		Weekly 22-
	Total	Num-ber	Per-cent	Num-ber	Per-cent	Num-ber	Per-cent	Num-ber	Per-cent	Num-ber	Per-cent	Num-ber	Per-cent	Num-ber	Per-cent	Num-ber
Total	1,273	805	100.	36	4.5	12	1.5	39	4.8	77	9.5	213	26.4	146	18.1	108
Professional	224	115	100.	6	5.2	1	0.9	2	1.8	6	5.2	23	20.0	15	13.0	17
Managerial and Official	101	34	100.	1	2.9	0	--	1	2.9	1	2.9	3	8.8	7	20.6	6
Clerical and Sales	331	229	100.	7	3.0	1	0.4	9	3.9	19	8.2	67	29.2	55	24.0	33
Clerk	124	94	100.	2	2.1	1	1.1	1	1.1	5	5.3	37	39.4	27	28.7	11
Office Worker	75	62	100.	2	3.2	0	--	3	4.9	9	14.5	16	25.8	16	25.8	11
Salesman	95	54	100.	2	3.7	--	--	4	7.4	5	9.2	11	20.4	11	20.4	7
Agent	30	16	100.	0	--	0	--	1	6.3	0	--	0	--	1	6.3	4
Peddler	7	4	100.	1	25.0	0	--	0	--	0	--	3	75.0	0	--	0
Service	155	116	100.	12	10.3	8	6.9	18	15.5	14	12.1	30	25.9	17	14.7	10
Agricultural and Kindred	1	1	100.	0	--	0	--	0	--	0	--	1		0	--	0
Skilled	383	265	100.	10	3.8	0	--	7	2.6	28	10.5	69	26.0	49	18.5	35
Semi-skilled	4	3	100.	0	--	0	--	0	--	1	33.3	1	33.3	0	--	1
Unskilled	72	42	100.	0	--	2	4.8	2	4.8	8	19.1	20	47.6	3	7.1	4
Miscellaneous	2	2	100.	0	--	0	--	0	--	0	--	0	--	0	--	2

a. One out of every five is retail.
b. One out of every eight is wholesale.
c. One out of every nine is export-import.
d. One out of every twelve conducts a service.

A better index of the amount of business involved in the various sub-divisions of trade is the ratio of those that employ only family members to those employing others:

a. The average number of employees varies from about six in the retail and export-import trade to about eight in the wholesale trade.
b. In service trade one out of every three employs only family members.
c. In retail trade one out of every five employs only family members.
d. In wholesale trade one out of every seven employs only family members.

25

by Major Occupational Groups
Earnings, Number, Percent
Summer, 1941

Earnings

| 25.99 | 26-29.99 | | 30-37.99 | | 38-45.99 | | 46-53.99 | | 54-61.99 | | 62-77.99 | | 78-109.99 | | 110-150 | | Not Reported |
Per-cent	Num-ber	Per-cent	Num-ber	Per-cent	Num-ber	Per-cent	Num-ber	Per-cent	Num-ber	Per-cent	Num-ber	Per-cent	Num-ber	Per-cent	Num-ber	Per-cent	Number
13.1	36	4.5	73	9.1	33	4.1	11	1.4	15	1.9	3	0.4	3	0.4	2	0.3	468
14.7	4	3.5	22	19.1	11	9.6	3	2.6	3	2.6	1	0.9	0	--	1	0.9	109
17.7	1	2.9	2	6.0	3	8.8	1	2.9	3	8.8	2	6.0	3	8.8	0	--	67
14.4	5	2.2	18	7.8	6	2.6	4	1.7	5	2.2	0	--	0	--	1	0.4	102
11.7	2	2.1	7	7.4	0	--	0	--	1	1.1	0	--	0	--	0	--	30
17.8	2	3.2	1	1.6	1	1.6	1	1.6	0	--	0	--	0	--	0	--	13
13.0	1	1.8	7	13.0	2	3.7	2	3.7	2	3.7	0	--	0	--	0	--	41
25.0	0	--	3	18.7	3	18.7	1	6.3	2	12.4	0	--	0	--	1	6.3	14
--	0	--	0	--	0	--	0	--	0	--	0	--	0	--	0	--	3
8.6	2	1.7	4	3.4	0	--	1	0.9	0	--	0	--	0	--	0	--	39
--	0	--	0	--	0	--	0	--	0	--	0	--	0	--	0	--	0
13.2	24	9.1	24	9.1	13	4.9	2	0.8	4	1.5	0	--	0	--	0	--	118
33.3	0	--	0	--	0	--	0	--	0	--	0	--	0	--	0	--	1
9.5	0	--	3	7.1	0	--	0	--	0	--	0	--	0	--	0	--	30
100.0	0	--	0	--	0	--	0	--	0	--	0	--	0	--	0	--	0

e. In export-import one out of every ten employs only family members.

In comparison with all retail concerns in New York City in 1939* the following ratios are observed:

a. Refugee retail concerns account for about one out of eight hundred.

b. Employees of refugee retail concerns account for one out of every four hundred employees.

The second largest category in number is manufacturing which accounted for one out of every three refugee concerns. The 290 refugee concerns which employed other than family members were engaged as follows:

* Retail Trade - New York - 1939, Table 17, Sixteenth Census of the United States, U. S. Department of Commerce, 1940.

TABLE 26

Interviewed Refugee Families in Which All Working Members Reported Weekly Earnings, Classified by Period of Arrival, by Number of Persons Working, by Combined Weekly Earnings, and by Medians

Number Working, Each Period	Total Families With One or More Workers	Families With All Working Members Reporting Weekly Earnings	Combined Weekly Earnings												Median Weekly Earnings Reported
			$8-11	$12-15	$16-19	$20-27	$28-35	$36-43	$44-51	$52-67	$68-83	$84-115	$116-147	$148 and over	
All Periods	719	419	22	64	36	67	72	38	35	43	19	14	4	5	$ 30.40
Period I	243	145	1	10	7	20	29	19	16	26	9	4	3	1	38.50
1 Working	98	74	1	9	7	20	19	4	6	7	1	1	—	—	26.00
2 Working	96	45	—	1	—	—	10	12	8	9	3	—	—	—	45.50
3 Working	29	14	—	—	—	—	—	3	2	6	3	2	—	—	54.50
4 Working	19	11	—	—	—	—	—	—	—	4	2	1	3	1	72.00
Period II	241	127	9	20	9	21	19	8	14	9	5	8	1	4	30.00
1 Working	103	73	9	19	8	16	12	2	5	—	1	—	—	1	20.00
2 Working	85	28	—	1	1	5	7	3	5	2	—	1	1	—	36.00
3 Working	34	17	—	—	—	—	—	3	3	6	3	2	—	2	58.50
4 Working	19	9	—	—	—	—	—	—	1	1	1	5	—	1	93.00
Period III	170	107	9	15	17	19	20	9	4	8	5	1	—	—	25.30
1 Working	82	59	7	15	15	9	8	1	1	2	—	1	—	—	18.00
2 Working	63	34	2	—	2	9	11	6	2	1	1	—	—	—	31.00
3 Working	20	10	—	—	—	1	1	1	—	4	3	—	—	—	60.00
4 Working	5	4	—	—	—	—	—	1	1	1	1	—	—	—	52.00
Period IV	65	40	3	19	3	7	4	2	1	—	—	1	—	—	15.50
1 Working	44	34	3	19	3	4	3	1	1	—	—	—	—	—	15.00
2 Working	18	5	—	—	—	3	1	1	—	—	—	1	—	—	26.50
3 Working	3	1	—	—	—	—	—	—	—	—	—	—	—	—	100.00
4 Working	—	—	—	—	—	—	—	—	—	—	—	—	—	—	—

a. One out of every four manufactured apparel.
b. One out of every eight was in some type of leather goods.
c. One out of every eight was in food manufacture.
d. One out of every thirteen was in the chemical industry.
e. One out of every fourteen was in the diamond and jewelry industry.

A better indication of the significance of this distribution is a comparison with the number and distribution of all manufacturing concerns in New York City in 1940.* The following facts stand out:

a. Refugee concerns account for not more than one out of every 150 manufacturing concerns.
b. In apparel manufacture refugee concerns also account for one out of every 150.
c. In chemical manufacture refugee concerns account for one out of every sixty.
d. In diamond and jewelry manufacture refugee concerns account for one out of every twenty-six.
e. In the manufacture of certain types of leather goods refugee concerns account for one out of every sixteen.
f. In the manufacture of candy for approximately one out of every ten.

A comparison of the number of employees of refugee manufacturing concerns with those of all manufacturers reveals:

a. All employees of refugee concerns in manufacture represent less than one percent of the total.
b. Employees of refugee chemical manufacturers represent one out of sixty-seven.
c. Employees of apparel manufacturers account for one out of every 150.
d. Employees of refugee leather manufacturers of belts, bags, and gloves account for one out of every sixteen.

---

* Industrial Directory of New York State, Table III, Number of Factories and Factory Employees in New York City According to Industry, Albany, 1940, pp. 857-60.

e. Employees of refugee diamond and jewelry concerns
   account for one out of every ten.
f. Employees of refugee candy manufacturers also account for one out of every ten.

It is of interest to relate the last two sets of facts
in appraising the relative importance of refugee manufacturing concerns.

a. Although refugee candy concerns account for one out
   of every ten candy manufacturers, they furnish employment to only one out of every thirty-four persons employed in the manufacture of candy.
b. Although refugee apparel manufacturers represent approximately 25 percent of all refugee manufacturing,
   it gives employment to only one out of every 150
   employees engaged in the manufacture of apparel.

TO WHAT EXTENT HAVE AMERICAN WORKERS BEEN DISPLACED?

On the basis of the facts noted above, it is clear that
among the estimated 35,000 refugee workers in New York
City who represent probably not more than one in every
hundred gainfully employed workers in New York City in
1940, there is very little likelihood of displacement of
American workers. Refugee entrepreneurs have not engaged
to any considerable degree in the large manufacturing industries. Although some refugee concerns have introduced
new products and developed new patents and processes
which have opened up some markets, new to America, they
have not to any appreciable degree offered competition to
already established New York business enterprises. They
have, on the other hand, given employment to some 9,000
workers of whom 6,000 are reported to be Americans. Thus
the question of the displacement of Americans by refugees
is largely hypothetical. It has a psychological base.

The position of the critic affects his judgment on the
adjustment of the refugee to the American labor market.
The older immigrant does not like to see the newer immigrant pushing him out. He forgets frequently that his
own immigrant status is still visible, or if it is hidden,
it is rarely more than three layers deep.

The professional whose job and whose income depends
upon general good business conditions which make possible

endowments to schools, colleges, and research institutions, fears the newcomer in time of depression. The physician, the architect, the designer, and the musician fear the competition of the newcomer whose skills are frequently equal to his own and sometimes available at lower cost.

The white collar worker does not like to see the refugee in jobs where he competes with him but wishes him in the unskilled groups. The unskilled group, in turn, feels the competition of the more educated refugee for jobs in his field.

When jobs are scarce there is a shifting of workers all down the line. The man with the Ph.D. in chemistry washes bottles in a laboratory, the former school teacher becomes a secretary, and the former secretary, a salesgirl. Since the unskilled are the largest single group of workers they are the ones who feel the pressure most.

In a depressed labor market, for the American out of a job, every foreigner who has a job seems to be a competitor. While the American accepts the fact of American competition because he is so used to it, he resents the seeming competition of the newcomer or that of any minority group -- racial, religious. Men object to women as competitors in business. The refugee, however, should not be held accountable for the inconsistency of our economic system which in time of contraction means that there are not enough jobs to go around, and that anyone who takes a job is ipso facto displacing someone else.

CONCLUSION

While this study does not pretend to be a comprehensive piece of economic research covering all types of refugee enterprises, nor to represent the facts as to the total amount of money invested by refugees in America and their contribution to the American economy, it does attempt to answer the questions of those people whose opinion is that all that the refugee has done in America is to take away jobs from Americans. The study has indicated the labor power that has been added, and the number of new skills now being taught to Americans.

The amount of competition involved in refugee business enterprises is so negligible both in terms of the number

of concerns and the number of people employed, that it
does not warrant the difficult and complicated analysis
of such factors as cost, quality, and current consumer
income which would be involved in determining the extent
to which these refugee concerns afford actual competition
to American business.

In terms of averages, based on the facts in the refugee
enterprise study, each refugee entrepreneur in business
has created a job for approximately seven American workers
in New York City. No data are available on the incalcula-
ble amount of additional business and employment created
by the refugee demand for housing, food, clothing, trans-
portation, amusement, etc.

The general fear of the competition of the refugee has
clearly no basis in fact. Not only is the problem local-
ized in New York City, but it is infinitesimal in size
when the number of employees in the labor market who have
come but recently from Europe is compared to all those
gainfully employed in the United States today.

APPENDIX I

A CHECK WITH THE FILES OF THE CAPITAL LOAN COMMITTEE

ON THE NUMBER OF ENTERPRISES

When the list of New York City enterprises was checked
with that of the files of the Capital Loan Committee of
the National Refugee Service, Inc., there were only 112
additional enterprises discovered out of a considerably
larger list. (This committee assists refugees in the
establishment of or in the carrying on of business enterprises which need only small loans to start them off or
keep them going.)

The great majority of these concerns, eighty-five, had
no employees but were mainly individual undertakings such
as peddling junk, candy, foodstuffs, neckties, etc.;
cleaning stores; operating newspaper stands, repair shops,
rooming houses; butchers, milliners, and photographers.
There was one art dealer, one coffee merchant, and one
printer, among them.

Seventeen of the twenty-one enterprises which employed
other than family members had fewer than five employees
each.

Of the four enterprises that had more than five employees each, two had 10 employees each and manufactured
gloves and jewelry.

Two enterprises that had more than ten employees each
made bags and costumes.

All four of these types of enterprises were well represented in the original refugee enterprise list.

The fact that this search yielded no clues to any
source that would indicate different types of businesses
or even any considerable number of businesses different
from those in the refugee enterprise list seems an added
support for the representativeness of the original list.

APPENDIX II

COMMITTEE FOR SELECTED SOCIAL STUDIES, Form #1 Enterprise #

I)
a) Individual enterprise? Partnership, refugees? Americans? Corporation? refugees?
b) Have you branches? If so, where:
c) Date of establishment?

II)

Type of enterprise	Product or Service	Raw materials & equipment bought in U.S.		Total production	
		% of total	app. value	Value	Volume
Finance					
Manufacturing					
Trade: retail					
" wholesale					
" export-import					
Service industries					
Professions					
Others					

III)

Number of Employees	Occupations of employees			
	Americans		Europeans	
	Number full time	Number part time	Number full time	Number part time
Professional				
Executive				
Sales				
Clerical				
Skilled				
Unskilled				
Domestic				

IV) Have you introduced a new product ( ), process ( ), patent ( )
a) Describe in general terms:

b) Do you export from the U.S.? If so, to which countries:
c) Approximate value ($) and volume of export:
d) Are you supplying markets developed by you before your immigration? Where?

V) a) Date of arrival: b) Vocation in Europe c) Vocations in U.S.
d) Number of dependents here: Employed: Unemployed: Specify:
e) Number of dependents working in your enterprise: , other enterprises
Name of interviewer address date

Give name and address of other employers: For additional information use other side:

HEALTH AREA MAP - BOROUGH OF MANHATTAN

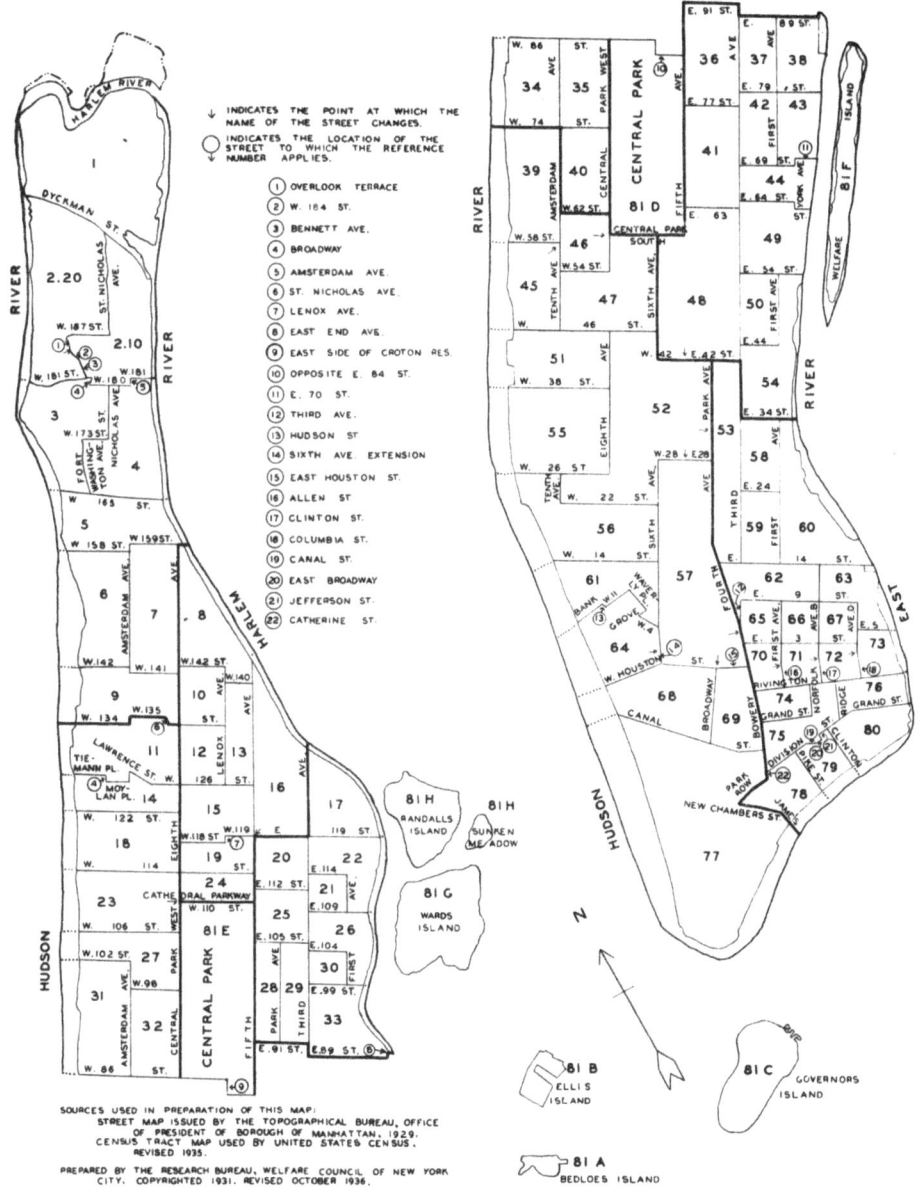

↓ INDICATES THE POINT AT WHICH THE NAME OF THE STREET CHANGES.
○ INDICATES THE LOCATION OF THE STREET TO WHICH THE REFERENCE NUMBER APPLIES.

1. OVERLOOK TERRACE
2. W. 184 ST.
3. BENNETT AVE.
4. BROADWAY
5. AMSTERDAM AVE.
6. ST. NICHOLAS AVE.
7. LENOX AVE.
8. EAST END AVE.
9. EAST SIDE OF CROTON RES.
10. OPPOSITE E. 84 ST.
11. E. 70 ST.
12. THIRD AVE.
13. HUDSON ST
14. SIXTH AVE. EXTENSION
15. EAST HOUSTON ST.
16. ALLEN ST
17. CLINTON ST.
18. COLUMBIA ST.
19. CANAL ST.
20. EAST BROADWAY
21. JEFFERSON ST.
22. CATHERINE ST.

SOURCES USED IN PREPARATION OF THIS MAP:
STREET MAP ISSUED BY THE TOPOGRAPHICAL BUREAU, OFFICE OF PRESIDENT OF BOROUGH OF MANHATTAN, 1929.
CENSUS TRACT MAP USED BY UNITED STATES CENSUS.
REVISED 1935.

PREPARED BY THE RESEARCH BUREAU, WELFARE COUNCIL OF NEW YORK CITY. COPYRIGHTED 1931. REVISED OCTOBER 1936.

Bei Fragen zur Produktsicherheit wenden Sie sich bitte an:
If you have any questions regarding product safety,
please contact:

Walter de Gruyter GmbH
Genthiner Straße 13
10785 Berlin
productsafety@degruyterbrill.com